CAMBRIDGE LIBRARY COLLECTION

Books of enduring scholarly value

Education

This series focuses on educational theory and practice, particularly in the context of eighteenth- and nineteenth-century Europe and its colonies, and America. During this period, the questions of who should be educated, to what age, to what standard and using what curriculum, were widely debated. The reform of schools and universities, the drive towards improving women's education, and the movement for free (or at least low-cost) schools for the poor were all major concerns both for governments and for society at large. The books selected for reissue in this series discuss key issues of their time, including the 'appropriate' levels of instruction for the children of the working classes, the emergence of adult education movements, and proposals for the higher education of women. They also cover topics that still resonate today, such as the nature of education, the role of universities in the diffusion of knowledge, and the involvement of religious groups in establishing and running schools.

Exercises in Idiomatic Italian

This innovative aid to the study of Italian was published in 1867 by Maria Francesca Rossetti (1827–76), the older sister of Dante Gabriel, William Michael and Christina. A scholar and teacher of Italian, she was later to publish *A Shadow of Dante*, a guide to the *Divine Comedy*, also reissued in the Cambridge Library Collection. Her purpose here, as she explains in her preface, is to demonstrate idiomatic Italian usage by providing short passages translated very literally into English, so that the 'unnatural' English phraseology demonstrates the correct Italian construction. The passages are to be translated back into Italian, with the help of some supplied vocabulary and an opening chapter which elucidates some of the more difficult aspects of Italian grammar, often by comparing Italian with French usage. The technique had long been used for Latin and Greek prose composition, but was innovatory for modern languages.

Cambridge University Press has long been a pioneer in the reissuing of out-of-print titles from its own backlist, producing digital reprints of books that are still sought after by scholars and students but could not be reprinted economically using traditional technology. The Cambridge Library Collection extends this activity to a wider range of books which are still of importance to researchers and professionals, either for the source material they contain, or as landmarks in the history of their academic discipline.

Drawing from the world-renowned collections in the Cambridge University Library and other partner libraries, and guided by the advice of experts in each subject area, Cambridge University Press is using state-of-the-art scanning machines in its own Printing House to capture the content of each book selected for inclusion. The files are processed to give a consistently clear, crisp image, and the books finished to the high quality standard for which the Press is recognised around the world. The latest print-on-demand technology ensures that the books will remain available indefinitely, and that orders for single or multiple copies can quickly be supplied.

The Cambridge Library Collection brings back to life books of enduring scholarly value (including out-of-copyright works originally issued by other publishers) across a wide range of disciplines in the humanities and social sciences and in science and technology.

Exercises in Idiomatic Italian

Through Literal Translation from the English

M ARIA F RANCESCA R OSSETTI

CAMBRIDGE
UNIVERSITY PRESS

CAMBRIDGE
UNIVERSITY PRESS

University Printing House, Cambridge, CB2 8BS, United Kingdom

Cambridge University Press is part of the University of Cambridge.
It furthers the University's mission by disseminating knowledge in the pursuit of
education, learning and research at the highest international levels of excellence.

www.cambridge.org
Information on this title: www.cambridge.org/9781108073318

This edition first published 1867
This digitally printed version 2014

ISBN 978-1-108-07331-8 Paperback

EXERCISES

IN

IDIOMATIC ITALIAN.

EXERCISES

IN

IDIOMATIC ITALIAN

THROUGH LITERAL TRANSLATION

FROM THE ENGLISH

BY

MARIA FRANCESCA ROSSETTI.

WILLIAMS AND NORGATE,

14, HENRIETTA STREET, COVENT GARDEN, LONDON;

AND

20, SOUTH FREDERICK STREET, EDINBURGH.

1867.

PREFACE.

I doubt whether any teacher of Italian will look into this book without at once pronouncing it absurd or pernicious — unless indeed he or she should happen to have met, in the same way as I have tried to meet it, the great difficulty in teaching languages. How shall pupils, after going through the grammatical course, be practised in writing, not English in Italian, but Italian itself? How shall their ear be trained to feel instinctively what is not Italian, even before they are sufficiently advanced to discover for themselves what is? How shall they be placed from the first in a position to write such translations as may need correction, but not re-writing?

As the result of a fairly successful attempt to solve these problems in the case of a pupil of my own, this little book is submitted to the judgment of English teachers and students of Italian. It consists of a hundred anecdotes selected from "Il Compagno del Passeggio campestre," the third edition of which appeared at Milan in 1830, published by the "Società tipografica de' classici italiani." These anecdotes being here translated into the most literal English of which grammar and sense will admit, their literal re-translation will result in the Italian of the original; and for this re-translation aid is given in three ways.

1. By bracketing words and clauses too utterly un-English for admission into the text, but intelligible as equivalent, when rendered into Italian, to the expressions used there. Any page of the book, opened at random, will exemplify this part of the system.

2. By giving in foot-notes such Italian words and expressions as cannot be thus represented, or require to be further dwelt on.

3. By copious elucidative notes.

The exercises thus constructed are mainly intended for the stage between the elementary grammatical course, and composition. Assuming the previous careful study of Mariotti's excellent, concise, sensible Grammar — or of any other good one — I seek to initiate English pupils into the mysteries of an idiom so different from their own by setting it before them in a form whose strangeness makes itself felt at once; at the same time securing the ear from becoming accustomed to unidiomatic Italian by making any but an idiomatic rendering impossible.

Three objections I foresee, and will endeavour to obviate.

1. "Is not this simply the Hamiltonian System?"

Certainly not simply. That system was never, so far as I know, applied to *writing* a foreign language. And mine differs from a Hamiltonian translation in at least one all-important point — that pre-supposing a knowledge of the grammar, it does not, while rendering word for word, falsify the emphasis of the sentence by retaining in English the position of the Italian conjunctive pronouns.

2. "Pupils will thus unlearn their own tongue while acquiring a foreign one; their Italian may be good, but what will their English be?"

Good too, as far as these exercises are concerned. The English here is never vulgar, and is much too odd to do the slightest harm. Who could possibly get into the way of saying, "done that he had it" instead of "when he had done it"?

3. "Pupils, once put into these leading-strings, will never be able to stand alone, but will remain just as incapable of composing in idiomatic Italian after this course as before it."

As far as my experience goes, the case is otherwise. By the end of the first part at latest they will be able to write tolerable letters, and to translate from other books alternately with the exercises in the second part, in which less help is given. All along their acquaintance with the grammar, especially with the rules relating to conjunctive and possessive pronouns, is taken for granted and closely tested. As a farther safeguard they should, on violating a rule, be required to correct the mistake, or to account for its correction. And when, to supersede or guide their use of the dictionary, one English word is bracketed as equivalent to another — as for example, "this course appeared to him *suitable* [*convenient*]," they should be led to perceive the connexion of meaning between the two words, and the primary sense of the bracketed one. — It will also be useful to dictate the corrected version, lest the ear should prove more retentive of wrong forms than of right ones.

A chapter is prefixed, in the hope of lessening the difficulties which even a careful study of the grammar will not have wholly removed. An alphabetical list of proper names, and an index to the notes, are subjoined. The anecdotes as they stand in the original are given in a Key, which may also prove useful as a reading-book.

P.S. The above was written, and the whole work ready for the press, some time before the appearance of Signor Toscani's excellent "Conversational Course," in which the plan of bracketing English for literal translation is also to some extent adopted. But his work is intended as a *first* Italian book, and does not therefore occupy the same ground as mine.

It is by an oversight that one or two anecdotes have been included, in which the authors appears somewhat lax as to truth.

CONTENTS.

A CHAPTER SUPPLEMENTARY TO THE GRAMMAR.

§ I. Of Words whose inflection implies the change of *c* and *g* into *ch* and *gh*.

General Principle. C and *g* once hard are always hard: i. e. *C* and *g* hard in a word capable of inflection remain hard throughout the inflections; and therefore become *ch* and *gh* when the inflection consists in changing the *a* or *o* which follows them into *e* or *i*.

This rule applies to nouns, adjectives, and verbs.

1) To nouns and adjectives ending in *ca, ga, co, go,* in respect of their plural.

2) To adjectives so ending in respect also of their superlative.

3) To verbs ending in *care, gare,* in respect of their future and conditional, and of certain persons in their 3 present tenses (i. e. pres. indic. and subj., and imperative).

Head 1. *Examples.* Monar*ca, chi*; le*ga, ghe;* fi*co, chi;* lun*go, ghi. Exceptions.* In *ca* and *ga*, none. In *co* and *go*, 2 classes. *Class* 1. 5 words having the penultimate syllable long: ami*co, ci;* nemi*co, ci;* por*co, ci;*

1

gre*co*, *ci;* ma*go* (magian) *gi.* (But *mago*, magician, follows the rule.) *Class* 2. Most words having the penult. short; as medi*co*, *ci.* (But dialogo, obbligo, parroco, and some others less common, follow the rule; and a few have both forms in the plural.)

HEAD 2. *Examples.* Ricco, *chissimo;* lar*ga*, *ghissima. Exceptions*, 2; Ami*co*, *chissimo* and *cissimo*; nemi*co, cissimo.* 2 others are exceptions to the Gen. Principle; a*cre*, *cerrimo;* inte*gro*, *gerrimo.*

HEAD 3. *Examples*, see Mariotti's Grammar, page 86 (or the verbs in *care* and *gare* as given in any grammar). *Exceptions,* none.

§ II. THREE RULES RESPECTING PERSONAL AND CONJUNCTIVE PRONOUNS.

1) Omit the nominative pronoun when you may, express it when you must: i. e. 1) When ambiguity would result from its omission; 2) When it requires to be emphasized.

2) Use conjunctive pronouns always when you may, personal pronouns only when you must: i. e. 1) After a preposition; 2) When the pronoun requires to be emphasized.

3) The conj. pron. *loro* always follows the verb. But as to all the rest — Place the conj. pron. before the verb when you may, after it when you must: i. e. In the infinitive, gerund, past participle without an auxiliary, 1st and 2nd persons imperative affirmative.

Abundant examples and many useful remarks will be found in Mariotti's or any good grammar. — The above rules are offered as simple and easily remembered formulæ, to guard beginners from incorrectness in composing or translating. But 1. and 3. are very far from exhaustive; the nom. pron. is often elegantly expressed, the conj. pron. placed after the verb, in other than the necessary cases; and the proficient will continually see reason to depart from the *may* of these rules, though never from the *must.*

§ III. Of the Passive Verb and the Particle Si.

Si, as a reflective and reciprocal pronoun, follows the rules of other conjunctive pronouns, and requires no special notice. We have here to do with it only as a particle imparting a passive signification to an active verb; in which character it is connected with one main difficulty of the language.

General Principle. A strong tendency to the passive voice pervades the Italian language. Hence this voice admits of far greater variety in form than is the case in French, which no less decidedly prefers the active voice; or in English, which stands between the two.

The Italian Passive Verb has 3 different forms.

1) The passive participle with the auxiliary essere, in all moods, tenses, and persons. (As in French and English.) Example: esser temuto, to be feared.

2) The pass. part. with the very peculiar auxiliary venire, in all moods except the imperative; in all *simple* tenses; in all persons. — Ex.: venir temuto, to be feared.

3) The active verb with the particle si prefixed, in all moods and tenses, the compounds being formed with essere; but only in the 3rd person. Ex. Temersi, to be feared: temendosi; temutosi or essendosi temuto. Si teme, si temono; si temeva, si temevano: si è temuto, si son temuti, &c.

Examples with Observations.

The difficulty referred to above is the construction of sentences in which the *action* rather than the *agent* is the subject of discourse. In French the vague nominative *on* with an active verb is employed: in English various forms — chiefly a passive verb with an impersonal nominative; in Italian also various forms — chiefly a passive verb of the 3rd class. The whole subject is so complicated that I can best hope to render it intelligible by subjoining a series of examples in all three languages, and explaining the Italian ones.

    ɪ. Sentences without an accusative.

1) On dit = It is said, *or* People say = Si dice.

Simply a pass. v. in the 3rd form; the literal translation of *it is said*, *it* being left out because in Italian impersonal nominatives almost universally, and pronominal noms. generally, are left out.

2) On dort ici = They are all asleep here = Qui si dorme.

Note first that the nom. in this sentence is really far less vague than in the last; it must necessarily be definite persons who are spoken of, though they are mentioned in an indefinite way. — Note, secondly, that here a *neuter* verb is expressed in a passive form, as is frequently the case when the nominative is indefinite. (A similar idiom exists in German: es wird getanzt und gespielt = people are dancing and playing.)

    ɪɪ. With an accusative of the 3rd person.

1) On le dit = So they say = Si dice.

This example is the same in Italian as Ex. I. 1.; the difference of meaning appears in the French and English, which here denote a reference to some previous assertion. Of course the Fr. acc. to an act. v. becomes the Ital. nom. to a pass. v. Apply what is said under Ex. I. 1. of pronominal noms.; and remember that the pass. v. constructed with si being of the 3rd pers only, all suppressed noms. must be understood in that person.

2). On la punira == She will be punished == Sara punita.

The 1st form of the pass. v. is here used, because si, being not only the passive particle, but also the reflective pronoun of the 3rd person, is avoided when the verb connected with it might be supposed reflected. Si punirà might mean *she will punish herself*.

3) On voit un homme == A man is seen == Si vede un uomo.

4) On voit deux hommes == Two men are seen == Si vedono due uomini.

Note the change in the number of the verb, consequent on the change of case implied in the change of voice.

III. With an accusative of the 1st or 2nd person.

1) On me récompensera == I shall be rewarded == Sarò ricompensato.

2) On vous blâme == People blame you, *or* You are blamed == Siete biasimato.

In these sentences the 3rd form is impossible, because it is of the 3rd person only.

IV. With a dative case of any person, and with any oblique case except the accusative.

1) On me défend cela == This is forbidden me == Ciò mi si proibisce *or* Ciò m'è proibito.

2) On lui fait cette aumône = This alms is given him = Gli si fa questa limosina.

3) On court chez vous = They are hurrying to your house = Si corre da voi.

Obviously the change of voice can affect no case but the nom. and acc.

v. With a reflected verb.

1) On se trompe souvent lorsqu'on s'applaudit de ses actions = We are often mistaken when we applaud our own doings = C'inganniamo *or* l'uomo s'inganna sovente applaudendo le proprie azioni.

2) On m'a volé ma bourse, et l'on se cache de moi = Some one has stolen my purse, and is hiding from me = Taluno m' ha rubata la borsa e si nasconde da me.

Reflected verbs not being susceptible of a change of voice are retained, and a nominative supplied according to the sense. 1) This assertion applies to mankind generally; the nom. is therefore noi or l'uomo. 2) This applies to an individual; the nom. is therefore uno, taluno, alcuno, qualcuno, &c. (All these but uno would be used in the pl. were it more appropriate to the sense.) — Note — for you will need to have done so when you come to translate and compose — that the first verb in this sentence is not reflected; but as the second is, and will consequently require a nom., the first verb also is put in the active voice, and the nom. expressed the first time, understood the second.

vi. With the adv. non, and the conjunctive prons. ci or vi, and ne.

1) On ne le dit pas = It is not said = Non si dice.

2) On y parle d'elle = She is spoken of there = Ci *or* vi si parla di lei.

3) On en demande = Some is asked for = Se ne chiede.

Non, ci and vi precede si; ne follows it and requires its euphonic change into se.

vii. With double conjunctive pronouns.

1) On lui en parla = They spoke to him about it = Gliene fu parlato.

2) On lui en donnera = Some will be given her = Gliene verrà dato.

These forms of the pass. v. are used with double pronouns for euphonic reasons.

viii. In compound tenses.

1) On a parlé de vous = You were talked of = Si è *or* Fu parlato di voi.

2) On me l'a dit = I have been told so = Mi è stato *or* Mi fu detto.

3) On nous avait parlé de lui = We had been spoken to about him = Ci era stato *or* Ci fu parlato di lui.

1) The 3rd form is the better here, as there is no acc., and only one pronoun. 2) But here, as there is an acc., it is inadmissible. 3) And here the 1st is better, as there are two pronouns. As a rule, use the 1st form in compound tenses unless you are quite certain to the contrary; it is never wrong, often exclusively right. — Note further in Ex. 2 and 3 the alternative of fu for è stato and era stato. This is allowed in the perfect and pluperfect to avoid the cumbrous double participle; and is especially to be preferred with verbs in are (Ex. 3), as in these the two participles rhyme.

§ IV. OF THE ITALIAN VERBS **Potere** TO BE-ABLE, **Volere** TO WILL, **Dovere** TO OWE; IN CONNEXION WITH THE ENGLISH VERBS *may, can; will; ought, must; shall.*

[Proficients in French need not read this section; to them it is sufficient to say that **potere, volere, dovere,** derived from the same Latin roots as *pouvoir, vouloir, devoir,* correspond with them both in rules and construction.

Students of German should read it, considering as they go on what points of difference and resemblance these Italian verbs present, when compared with the German auxiliary verbs of mood. Though the one language is of Latin, the other of Teutonic origin, many points of resemblance will be perceived, one especially, viz. that in neither language are these verbs defective, except as respects the imperative.]

Why do English students so continually fail to master these Italian verbs? Because their attention has not been directed to the following points.

I. **Potere, volere, dovere,** are 1) irregular verbs: 2) of Latin origin: 3) never auxiliary: 4) not defective: 5) varying more or less in meaning according to the tense employed.

II. Their principal English equivalents are, 1) perfectly anomalous verbs: 2) of Teutonic origin: 3) three of them often auxiliary: 4) all defective, which causes, *a)* That one English form may correspond to two or more Italian: *b)* that the Eng. verb must often be supplemented in some of its moods and tenses by another verb, whereas the Ital. verb remains the same: *c)* that the tense used in English is not always the same as that required in Italian.

These three, *shall*, *will*, *may*, are frequently mere auxiliaries, *shall* and *will* of the future tense, *may* of the subjunctive and potential moods. As such they are not translated separately from the principal verb, nor have we here anything to do with them. When more than auxiliaries they are emphasized in English, or else capable of having some other verb substituted for them. Examples will be found in the proper place.

I proceed to give the three Italian verbs, with their English equivalents, and reasoned examples wherever necessary. The English tense and person do not always grammatically correspond with the Italian; rather they are idiomatically equivalent.

I. Inf. Pres. **Potere** = **to be-able.** (Can, May.) Gerund. Potendo = being-able. Past Part. Potuto = been-able.

Infin. Perf. Aver potuto = to have been-able. Compound Gerund. Avendo potuto = having been-able.

Indic. Pres. Posso = I can, am-able; I may, am-permitted.

1) **Posso** andare = I *can* go. 2) **Può** essere = it *may* be; **non può** essere = it *cannot* be. 3) **Posso** farlo? = *may* I do it? **Puoi** uscir con tua sorella = you *may* go out with your sister. 4) **Posso** averlo fatto = I *may* have done it.

The present tense, 1) expresses power: 2) possibility: 3) asks and grants permission: 4) With the perf. infin it expresses a conjecture or conclusion.

Imperf. Poteva = I could, was-able.

1) Da giovane io **poteva** far venti miglia alla volta
= when young I *could* walk twenty miles at a time.
2) **Potevi imparare** allora, ma non hai voluto = you
could then *have learned*, but you would not.

The imperf. 1) expresses a past prolonged or habitual
power or possibility. (Note this first *could*, and see note
on imperf. subj.) 2) Followed by a negative clause it
is sometimes used instead of the past conditional.

PRETERIT. Potei = I could, was-able.

1) L'implorammo a soccorrerci, ma non **potè**, man-
candogli i mezzi = we entreated him to aid us, but
he *could* not for want of means. 2) **Potè** salvare il suo
bambino dall' annegare = he *was-able* to save (i. e. he
succeeded in saving) his infant son from drowning.

1) Power or powerlessness: 2) success or non-suc-
cess, in an action or enterprize entirely past. (Note this
second *could*, and see note on imperf. subj. — See also
note on perf. indic.)

PERFECT. Ho potuto = I have been-able.

Much the same senses as the preterit, but with
somewhat more bearing on the present. If I say, Non
potè salvare il figlio dal fuoco, my main idea is the
misery of the baffled effort at the time; if I say, Non
l' **ha potuto** salvare, I am thinking also of the perma-
nent loss sustained.

PLUPERF. Aveva potuto = I had been-able.

FUTURE. Potrò = I shall-be-able.

CONDIT. Potrei = I could, should-be-able; might.

1) **Potrei aiutarvi se mel permetteste** = I *could* help
you if you would let me. 2) **Potrebbe darsi** = it *might* be.

1) Power under certain conditions. (Note this third
could, and see note on subj. imperf.) 2) Chance or possibility.

Future anterior. Avrò potuto = I shall-have been-able.

1) Corro a servirvi; e se l'avrò potuto fare vi scriverò subito = I hasten to serve you, and if *I shall-have been-able* to do it will write to you instantly. 2) Non mi ricordo troppo quella circostanza; ma se allora non v'aiutai, sarà che non l'avrò potuto fare = I do not clearly remember that circumstance; but if I did not then help you, it must have been that *I could* not do so.

1) In Italian as in English an admissible, but unusual and cumbrous form. 2) See here the chief use of this tense; both futures are much used to express a conjecture or conclusion.

Past Condit. Avrei potuto = I could have (done) *or* should-have been-able (to do); might have (done).

See note 2 on indic. imperf. — The sentence there given might equally have been; Avresti potuto imparare allora &c.

N.B. I could have done it is never rendered by potrei averlo fatto. (See note on past condit. of dovere.)

Subj. Pres. (che) Possa = (that) I can, be-able; may.

1) Credete ch'io possa trovarlo in casa? do you think I *may* find him at home?

2) Non credo ch'ei lo possa fare, I do not think he *can* do it.

1) Chance or possibility. 2) Power.

Imperf. (che) Potessi = (that) I could, were-able.

Andrei se potessi = I would go if I *could*.

Note this fourth *could;* compare it carefully with the others; and when you have to translate *I could,* think whether it means "*I was-able* at a past time" (imperf. or pret. indic.), "*I should-be-able* under certain conditions" (conditional), or "if *I were-able* such a result would follow" (imperf. subj.)

Perfect. (che) Abbia potuto = (that) I have been-able.

Pluperf. (che) Avessi potuto = (that) I had been-able.

II. Volere = to will. (Will.)

It must be remembered that besides the irreg. defective, neut. and sometimes aux. v. *will*, there is in English the act. and reg. v. *to will*, also practically defective, only a few of its parts being ever used. It is found almost exclusively in moral and religious writings, in such sentences as the first of the following examples.

Will and *would*, used in rendering **volere**, are never mere auxiliaries.

Infin. Pres. Volere = to will; to intend; (occasionally) to wish.

1) Per liberarsi da un vizio non bastano i soli desiderj; bisogna volerlo fortemente, o non se ne verrà mai a capo = to get rid of a fault mere wishes are not sufficient; we must *will* it strongly, or we shall never succeed. 2) Corre gran distanza dal voler fare al fare = there is a wide distance between *intending* and doing.

Gerund. Volendo = willing; wishing, wanting; purposing, intending.

1) **Volendolo** con animo risoluto ci riuscirai senza fallo = by *willing* it with a resolute mind you will assuredly succeed. 2) S'è-ritirato presto, **volendo** compiacere al padre = he went away early, *wishing, wanting*, to please

his father. 3) Il generale, **volendo** tentar l'assalto, ordinò ai soldati di tenersi in pronto = the general, *purposing*, *intending*, to attempt an assault, ordered the soldiers to hold themselves in readiness. P<small>AST</small> P<small>ART</small>. Voluto (primarily) = willed, chosen; but it must be rendered according to the tense. I<small>NFIN</small>. P<small>ERF</small>. Aver voluto = to have willed, wished, wanted, intended.

Non basta **averlo voluto**, bisognava farlo = it is not enough to have *wished*, *intended*, it, you ought to have done it. C<small>OMP</small>. G<small>ERUND</small>. Avendo voluto = having willed. Much less used than volendo. I<small>NDIC</small>. P<small>RES</small>. Voglio = I will, am resolved, choose, please; I purpose, intend; I want; it is my will, pleasure; I will have, take; I will have (it), i. e. choose it to be; I would have (it), i. e. want it to be.

1) **Voglio** scrivergli = I *will, am resolved to, purpose to, intend to*, write to him. 2) Lo fa perchè lo **vuol** fare = he does it because he *will, chooses to,* do it. 3) Che **vuoi**? what *do* you *want*? what *would* you *have*? 4) Qual **volete** di queste frutta? **Voglio** l'arancio = which of these fruits *will* you *have*? I *will have* the orange. 5) Questo nastro mi piace, ne **voglio** tre braccia = I like this ribbon, I *will take* three yards. 6) Perche l'avete ordinato così? Perchè così lo **voglio** = why have you arranged it so? Because so I *will, choose to, have* it. 7) **Voglio** ch'ei ci vada = I *will have* him go there. 8) Ti **voglio** modesto sì, ma fermo e risoluto nel bene = I *would have* you, *want* you *to be,* modest indeed, but firm and resolute in what is right. I<small>DIOMATIC</small>. Si **vuol** parlargli con dolcezza = *it will be right* to speak gently to him.

Imperf. Voleva = I wished, wanted; I meant; I would have (it), i. e. wanted (it) to be. 1) Essa **voleva** parlarmi, ma io l'evitai = she *wanted, wished,* to speak to me, but I avoided her. 2) **Volevamo** passar la mattinata a studiare, ma tuo fratello ce l'ha impedito = we *wanted, meant,* to pass the morning in study, but your brother hindered us. 3) Lo **volevamo** costumato, onde abbiam sempre allontanato da lui i cattivi esempi = we *would have* his morals pure, therefore we kept him from bad examples.

This tense expresses mere wishes and intentions, and implies failure, except in cases like Ex. 3, where it expresses a prolonged and habitual will.

Preterit. Volli = I would, I willed: I was resolved, determined; I chose, pleased; it was my will, pleasure; I would have (it), i. e. wanted (it) to be.

1) Il re **volle** punir l'un reo e perdonare all' altro = *it was the king's will, pleasure,* to punish one of the criminals and pardon the other. 2) **Volli** trovarla, e l'ho trovata = I *was resolved, determined,* to find her, and I have found her. 3) Lo **volli** fare vostro malgrado = I *would* do it in spite of you. 4) Lo **volemmo** corretto d'un sì brutto vizio, onde l'abbiam castigato = we *would have* him, *wanted* him *to be,* corrected of so hateful a fault, wherefore we have chastised him.

This tense expresses will, resolution, determination, and implies success.

Perfect. Ho voluto = I would, &c.

L'ho pregato e ripregato, ma non mi **ha voluto** sentire = I begged and begged him, but he *would* not hear me.

The note on the perf. of **potere** applies also here.

Pluperf. Aveva voluto.

Much less used than **voleva.**

FUTURE. Vorrò = I shall-please, like, choose, be-willing.

1) Certo, lo potrà fare se vorrà = he will certainly be able to do it if he *likes*, *chooses*. 2) Vedrete che non **vorranno** ubbidirvi = you will see they *will* not *choose*, *be-willing*, to obey you.

This tense is scarcely ever used in the 1st person, occasionally in the 2nd, often in the 3rd.

CONDITIONAL. Vorrei = I would, wish, want; I should-wish, should-like, would-have; I would have (it), i. e. wish (it) were.

1) Oh quanto **vorrei** vederlo! = how I *should-like* to see him! 2) **Vorrebbe** comprarsi una grammatica, ma non ha danari = he *wants*, *wishes*, *would-like*, to buy himself a grammar, but has no money. 3) **Vorrei** se potessi = I *would* if I could. 4) Nol **vorrei** ancor che me l'offrisse in dono = I *would* not *have* it if he would make me a present of it. 5) Ti **vorrei** men presuntuoso e più applicato a' tuoi doveri = I *would have you, wish you were*, less conceited and more attentive to your duty. 6) **Vorresti** farmi sentire il tuo componimento? == *would you be so kind as* to read me your work?

This tense is in continual use; it expresses wishes, and implies obstacles and defects. — With a negative (Ex. 4) it sometimes expresses will. — It is also (Ex. 6) used as a courteous form of request.

FUTURE ANTERIOR. Avrò voluto = I shall-have willed, pleased, chosen, determined, meant.

Avrà voluto insinuarvi di partire = he *must have meant* to hint to you to go.

The conjectural fut. ant. (See note 2 on this tense in **potere**.)

Past Condit. Avrei voluto = 1 should-have wished, liked, (to do); should-have chosen; would have (done).

1) **Avresti voluto** leggerlo? = *would* you *have wished, liked,* to read it? 2) **Avrebbe voluto** piuttosto il Dante che il Tasso = he *would-have liked, chosen,* the Dante rather than the Tasso. 3) **L'avremmo voluto** ricompensare, ma era già partito = we *would have* rewarded him, but he was gone.

The imperf. may often be used instead of this tense.
— Be sure you never translate *I would have done it* by **vorrei averlo fatto**; for this means *I wish I had done it*. (See also note on past condit. of **dovere**.)

Subj. Pres. (che) Voglia = (that) I will, be-willing, choose, please.

1) Sperate ch'ei **voglia** farvi questa finezza? = do you hope he *will* do you this kindness? 2) Basta che tu **voglia** = it is enough that you *be-willing*.

Imperf. (che) Volessi = (that) I would, were-willing, wanted, chose, meant, would-have (it), i. e. wanted (it) to be.

1) Se **voleste** rivederlo tutto andrebbe bene = if you *would* see him again all would be well. 2) Se avessi saputo che lo **voleste** così, così appunto l'avrei fatto = had I known that you *wished, wanted,* it so, just so would I have done it.

Note the recurrence of *would,* as before of *could;* and see note on subj. imperf. of **potere**.

Perfect. (che) Abbia voluto = (that) I have chosen, pleased, been-willing, wanted, meant.

Non credo ch'ella **abbia voluto** offendervi = I do not think she *meant* to offend you.

Pluperf. (che) Avessi voluto = (that) I had chosen, pleased, wanted, been-willing, meant.

Se tu l'avessi voluto l'avresti già fatto = if you *had chosen* to do it you would have done it by this time.

III. Dovere = Ought, must, should.

Dovere is *to owe*, primarily *money* &c, secondarily *duty* &c. In the primary sense it is peculiar only as being irregular, and wanting the imperative; it therefore offers no difficulty, and is not treated of here. In the secondary sense it is chiefly represented by the defective verb *ought*, which is really nothing else than the older form of *owed*, and was once so used: for example, as the translation of S. Matthew's Gospel originally stood, "*owed* him ten thousand talents" was "*ought* him." It is represented also by *should*, used as a synonym of *ought;* this indeed is its etymological value, as being from the old German ſcolan, i. e. ſollen, *to owe*. So far there is therefore no discrepancy of sense; the difficulties arise. 1) from **dovere** corresponding also sometimes to *must*, &c. 2) from the anomalous construction of both *ought* and *must*.

INFIN. PRES. Dovere = to be in duty bound; to be-obliged; to have-to (do). Oh quanto mi spiace **doverci** perder tanto tempo! = how sorry I am *to have, be-obliged*, to waste so much time over it!

GERUND. Dovendo = being-bound, obliged; having-to (do).

Dovendo badare a parecchi affari ho passata la mattina in casa = *having to* attend to several matters I have spent the morning at home.

PAST PART. Dovuto = been-obliged.

INFIN. PERF. Aver dovuto = to have been-obliged, had-to (do).

2

L' aver dovuto rifiutare una tal richiesta mi rincresce molto = *to have been-obliged, had*, to refuse such a request grieves me much.

Comp. Gerund. Avendo dovuto = having been-obliged, had-to (do).

Much less used than **dovendo**.

Indic. Pres. Debbo = I must; I have-to; I am-to; I am-bound-to; it is my duty to; I must (have done it).

1) Non ci **debbo** andare = I *am* not *to* go there.
2) Ci **devi** provveder subito = you *must* see to it directly.
3) **Debbo** passar da un amico, e passerò prima da voi = I *have-to* call at a friend's, and will first call at your house.
4) Voi gliel comandate, e **deve** eseguirlo senza replica = you order him to do it, and *he must, he is-bound-to, it is his duty to*, do it without a word.
5) Qual di voi due **deve** venir meco? = which of you two *is-to* come with me?
6) I figli **debbono** ubbidire ai genitori = children *must* obey their parents.
7) **Debbo** averlo detto, poichè ve ne ricordate = I *must* have said it, since you remember it.

This tense implies: 1) moral obligation; 2) necessity imposed by circumstances or by another's will; 3) in connexion with the perf. infin. (Ex. 7) a conclusion from premises. *Ought* and *should*, though admissible renderings in Ex. 4 and 6, would be somewhat weak; in this tense moral obligation is regarded as moral necessity, and neglect of it is not contemplated.

Imperf. Doveva = I should, ought-to, have (done); I was-bound, it was my duty, place, to (do); I was-to.

1) Tua madre **doveva correggerti** da piccina, è ora troppo tardi = your mother *should, ought-to, have corrected* you when little, it is now too late.
2) Ci ho già pensato, e **doveva** pensarci io, non tu = I have

settled it, and *it was my duty, place*, not yours, to settle it. 3) Ho soccorso quel poverello, ma non so se doveva farlo. Sì certo, dovevate farlo = I have assisted that poor man, but know not whether I *ought-to have done it*. Yes, assuredly, *it was your duty, you were bound*, to do it. 4) So che dovevano impararlo, perchè non l'abbiano imparato non lo so = I know they *were to* learn it, why they have not learned it I know not.

This tense, in contrast with the present, expresses, 1) moral duty regarded as matter not of necessity, but of choice; 2) requirement, but not compulsion, resulting from circumstances or from another's will. It is therefore used when the duty or requirement has not been fulfilled (Ex. 1, 4). Like the imperf. of potere and volere, it is used (Ex. 1, 3, 4) instead of the past condit.; therefore one great difficulty connected with it is explained in a note on that tense.—In Ex. 2. doveva pensarci is rendered *it was my duty to settle it*, not *I ought to have settled it;* this last form is in English equivalent to the past condit., and always implies either neglect of duty (Ex. 1) or doubt respecting duty (doveva in Ex. 3).

PRETERIT. Dovei = I was-obliged, had, to (do it).

I ribelli dovettero deporre le armi = the rebels *were-obliged, had*, to lay down their arms.

This tense expresses an entirely past compulsion or necessity.

PERFECT. Ho dovuto = I have been-obliged, had, to (do it).

1) Ho dovuto con mio gran rammarico congedar quel servo = I *have been-obliged*, to my great regret, to dismiss that servant. 2) Ho dovuto alfine prestargli i denari = I *had* at last *to* lend him the money.

2 *

See note on this tense in **potere**; and observe (Ex. 2) that it is often rendered by the English imperf.

PLUPERF. Aveva dovuto = I had been-obliged, had, to (do it). Much less used than the pret. and perf.

FUTURE. Dovrò = I shall-be-obliged, have, to (do). 1) In tal caso **dovrà** chiederle scusa = in that case he *will-have to* beg her pardon. 2) Se voi negligete un affare sì importante **dovrò** badarci io = if you neglect business so important I *shall be-obliged, have,* to attend to it.

CONDIT. Dovrei = I should, I ought-to; I should-be-obliged, should-have, to (do). 1) **Dovrebbe** applicarsi davvero allo studio, ed ecco che passa giornate intere a divertirsi = he *ought-to, should,* apply in good earnest to his studies, and here he is passing whole days in mere amusement. 2) **Dovrei** correre come il vento per arrivarci a tempo, onde rinunzio ad andarci = I *should-have to* run like the wind to get there in time, therefore I give up going.

This tense expresses both duty and necessity, and implies neglect or non-performance.

FUT. ANT. Avrò dovuto = I shall-, must-have been-obliged. 1) Arriverete troppo tardi per soccorrerlo; vedrete che **avrà dovuto** disfarsi di tutto = you will arrive too late to help him; you will see he *has been-obliged* to part with all his things. 2) Se ha venduto quell' anello, l'**avrà dovuto** vendere per forza = if he has sold that ring, he *must-have been-forced* to sell it.

The fut. ant. is rendered by the perf. in Ex. 1, the two futures in succession not being the Engl. idiom.

— Ex. 2 is the conjectural fut. ant. (see note on this tense in **potere**.)

PAST CONDIT. Avrei dovuto = I should, ought-to, must, have (done it); it would have been my duty, I should have had, to (do it).

1) **Avrei dovuto serbar** con più cura il manoscritto da voi affidatomi = I *should, ought-to have taken* more care of the M.S. you entrusted to me. 2) **Avrebbero dovuto nutrire** il vecchio padre = they *ought to have maintained* their old father. 3) In caso che avesse perduto il mio libro **avrebbe dovuto** comprarmene un altro = in case he had lost my book *it would have been his duty* to buy me another. 4) **Avrei· dovuto comprar** questo dizionario quando non aveste favorito prestarmelo = I *must have bought, should have had to buy*, this dictionary, had you not kindly lent it me.

This tense expresses (Ex. 1 and 2) neglected duty; (Ex. 3) conditional duty; (Ex. 4) conditional necessity. *N.B.* You have seen (**potere** and **volere**, past condit.) that *I could, would, have done it*, is equivalent to *I should-have been-able, willing, to do it;* i. e. that the imperf. tense with the perf. infin. is equivalent to the past condit. with the pres. infin. In rendering the verb **dovere** it is peculiarly necessary to understand the former of these two constructions, because (except in cases like Ex. 3) it is the only construction. There is this great difference between *could, would,* and *ought, must;* the two former can, the two latter cannot, be by themselves used in reference to the past. We say "he *would* leave this place *last week* in spite of me; I *could* lift this weight *yesterday*, today I find it impossible": — while on the other hand we say, not "I *ought to help* you *yesterday*," but "I *ought to have helped* you"; to which the Ital.

equivalent is not the literal **dovrei avervi assistito**, but **avrei dovuto assistervi**, i. e. word for word = *I should-have owed to help you.* — The case of *must* is still more complicated. We say, not "he *must* leave this place *last week*, because he was sent for", but "he *was-obliged to* leave"; this is the Ital. pret. **dovè**. — "He *must have left* this place *last week*, even had he not done so earlier"; this is the Ital. past condit. **avrebbe dovuto**. "He *must have left* this place *last week*, as he has not been seen since Saturday", this is the Ital. perf. **ha dovuto**, or the conjectural future **avrà dovuto**, according to the greater or less certainty of the conclusion; the literal **deve aver lasciato** is also used in this case.

SUBJ. PRES. (che) **Debba** = that I ought-to, should; am-to.

1) **Vi pare che ciò si debba risolvere?** = do you think this *should, ought to*, be resolved on? 2) **Il maestro non ha deciso che tu debba esser punito** = the master has not determined that you *are-to* be punished.

IMPERF. (che) **Dovessi** = (that) I should, ought-to.

Se dovessi cangiar di sistema mio padre me l'avrebbe fatto sapere = if I *ought-to* change my way of going on my father would have let me know.

Respecting the recurrence of *ought*, apply note on this tense in **potere**.

PERF. (che) **Abbia dovuto** = (that) I have been-obliged, had, to (do); must have (done).

Mi figuro che a quest'ora egli abbia dovuto pronunziarsi = I conclude that by this time he *has been-obliged, has had, to settle, must have settled*, the matter.

PLUPERF. (che) **Avessi dovuto** = (that) I had been-obliged, had, to (do); need have (done).

Non crederei che avessero dovuto partire avanti lunedì scorso = I should not think they *had been-obliged, had had, to start, need have started,* before last Monday.

Observe that the verb **dovere** is not the only equivalent to *must, ought,* &c.; the impers. verb **bisognare** with the subj. is also used, especially for *must.* 1) Bisogna che vi si sottometta = he *must* submit to it. 2) Bisognava spiegarvi meglio = you *should* have explained yourself more clearly. 3) Bisognerà andarci di buon ora = we *shall have* to go there early.

IV. Of shall.

Shall, should, have no corresponding Ital. verb (except, as you have seen, when *should* is synonymous with *ought*). Even when not *mere* auxiliaries they must be rendered by the fut., condit., or subj. imperf. of the verb with which they are connected; the emphasis being conveyed by the tone of voice, or supplied by the use of an adverb or expletive.

1) You *shall* go, that I am determined = andrete, così voglio. 2) He *shall* not do it while he is under me = non lo farà, no, mentre mi starà soggetto. 3) He can scarcely come in such weather; if however he *should,* tell him I did not expect him = È difficile che venga con questo tempo; se mai però venisse, ditegli ch' io non l'aspettava. 4) If they *should* wish for greater security, I pledge myself = se poi volessero maggior sicurtà, mi fo mallevadore io.

EXERCISES.

1. Judgment[1] of Phocion.

Antipater, one of the successors of Alexander the Macedonian, was a great admirer of Phocion Athenian, a man of such probity that there was not any who surpassed him. In sign of esteem and through desire of being useful to him, that prince made to Phocion most generous offers, which were by him refused with the most resolute constancy. It appeared well however to his friends to make him reflect that, if not for himself, it was always *beneficial*[2] that he should accept them for his sons. But Phocion, *whose*[3] paternal love was guided by wisdom, to such *hints* [*insinuations*] answered: "If my sons *are to*[4] resemble me, that which they have will suffice them, because *it was able*[5] to suffice also to me: if *however they want to be dissolute*[6], *I must not*[7] leave them the means of satisfying their caprices."

[1] Sentenza.   [2] giovevole.   [3] il cui.   [4] debbono.   [5] potè.   [6] poi vogliono essere scostumati.   [7] non debbo.

Questions and Notes.

[2] From what verb is giovevole formed?   [4] In what sense is the verb dovere used the first time? [It implies something that will happen beyond the control or foresight of the speaker.]   [7] And the

second time? [A moral obligation.] To what German verb does
it answer? [Sollen.] ⁶What is the force of s in scostumati?
[That of dis in English.] To what French word does costumi
answer? [Mœurs.]

2. The merciful ¹ Lion.

At the *expiration*² of the seventeenth century,
*there*³ fled from the park of the Grand Duke of Tus-
cany a lion. Let every one think what was the alarm
of the Florentines wherever might pass the wild beast.
A mother who clasped in her arms an infant, meets it,
and *rapt out of*⁴ herself, lets fall to the ground her
son, whom the lion *bites*⁵ by the dress and having-
held him suspended *continues its way* [*follows the road*].
The mother, at such a spectacle, forgets herself, pursues
the wild beast, and *having-come-up with it*⁶, throws
herself at its feet, *outstretches*⁷ the arms, and the bosom
panting and with the flames in the eyes, "Return me",
she cries, "return me the son." The lion which had
suspended the step, looks at her, and *as if*⁸ it venerated
in her the love of mother, *lays down*⁹ softly the prey
without the slightest *injury*¹⁰, and continues its steps.

The artists have taken the care to transmit to the
posterity this memorable event.

¹ pietoso. ² spirare. ³ Omit *there*. ⁴ rapita a. ⁵ addenta.
⁶ raggiuntala. ⁷ allarga. ⁸ quasi. ⁹ depone. ¹⁰ offesa.

¹From what noun is pietoso formed, and what is its literal
meaning? ³Why is *there* omitted? [It serves in English to enable
the verb to precede the nominative; in Italian it is not necessary,
the genius of the language allowing of this transposition whenever
convenience, harmony or emphasis requires it.] ⁵Addentare, to
seize with the teeth; from dente. ⁷From what adj. is allargare

formed? [Largo.] Then what position of the arms does it indicate?
[9] What is deponere or deporre in its literal meaning? Which of
the two meanings is the primary one? [10] Offesa is what? Shew
the difference between this word and the Engl. *injury*. What is
the Ital. ingiuria? [Insult.]

3. THE MOTHER VICTIM OF HER LOVE.

When happened [1] the horrible earthquake of Messina,
the lord Marquis of Spadara was enough happy to be
able to find safety near the port, running with his wife
suspended and *fainting* [2] between his arms. There he
met *with* [3] a boat in which he deposited the precious
burden [4].

It was then that the Marchioness *came to herself* [5],
opened her eyes, turned them around; an inexpressible
uneasiness depicted itself on her face, she untied [6] the
tongue and enquired *for* [*of*] the son: "Ah, dear friend",
replied to her, weeping, her husband, "one had not
time to think but of you." "One sees well," resumed
the Marchioness agitated, "that you are not a mother;"
and this said, she got up impetuously, resolved to
return home. The husband opposed himself, she insisted;
he withstood to her the passage, and she threw herself
at his feet, and conjured him that it should be permitted
her to *follow* [*second*] her heart. It was needful then
that the husband should employ the force; but in the
act that he turned himself to give a command, she
escaped from his hand, and ran like the lightning to
the palace which subsisted still in midst of the sur-
rounding ruins.

She arrived at the room of the son, whom she found
immersed in the most placid sleep. She took him,

clasped him to her bosom, loaded him with her kisses, bathed him with her *tears* [7], and with her treasure ran to the staircase . . . . Why must I proceed? . . . .

She felt vacillate under the feet the first stair, withdrew the step, and saw it precipitate under her *eyes* [*looks*]. She re-entered into the apartment, pursued by the horrid shock [8]: the ceiling was splitting itself, the beams were tottering [9]; she fled from room to room, arrived at last at a window. From there she presented the son to the affrighted people; invoked succour, pity; but in the midst of the screams, of the tears, of the prayers, yields the pavement, the wall precipitates, and the most tender of mothers with her son at the bosom . . . .

[2] svenuta.   [3] raggiunse.   [4] fardello.   [5] rinvenne.   [6] snodò. [7] pianto.   [8] scossa.   [9] crollavano.

[1] Why does this verb precede its nominative? [Because the nom. consists of several words.]   [2] Why is the past or passive, instead of the gerund or active, participle employed here? [Because it is the genius of the Italian language to regard persons as passive, and actions as complete at the time to which the verb refers. This is a matter to which your special attention should be directed; it would take up too much room to subjoin a note every time this substitution takes place, but you should never pass it over without accounting for it, till practice has rendered it familiar.] [6] What noun is the root of the verb snodare? [Nodo.]   [7] Why pianto rather than lagrime? [It expresses more abundant weeping, and is often far more idiomatic.]   [8] What verb is the root of scossa? [Scuotere, scosso.]

---

4. The Conflagration overcome by Maternal Affection.

In a conflagration *happening* [1] *by* [2] night to a rustic house called la Garenne, in the parish Duplessis-

Praslin, a woman of twentysix years wakes *almost*[3] in midst of the flames. In that horrible moment she thinks not except of a son *five years old* [*of a lustre*], who slept in a neighbouring room: this is all her good; the rest is nothing for her. She *rushes down* [*precipitates*] from the bed, and throws herself against the door which splits. *Eddies*[4] of smoke and of flames arrest her for an instant, but avail not to detain her. She cannot *longer*[5] walk on the floor: it behoves her to *rush*[6] from a beam that smokes to another that burns, and *wander*[7] in a furnace; she seeks, finds, seizes her son, presses him to her bosom, traverses the fire and *escapes* [*saves herself*].

Several were *busied*[8] in snatching from the flames the *remnants*[9] of her fortune: she passed in the midst without looking at them; she saw not except her son. With this pledge between her arms, with her eyes immovable *on* [*in*] him, she ran *even*[10] to the half of a field, rapt out of herself. *Failed to her all of a sudden the powers*[11], she fell to earth *swooning*[12], but with her treasure always strained to her bosom. She was thus transported to the village, where there was employed every means to revive her.

---

[1] accaduto.　[2] di.　[3] quasi.　[4] vortici.　[5] piu.　[6] slanciarsi. [7] ravvolgersi.　[8] affaccendati.　[9] avanzi.　[10] sino.　[11] le mancarono tutto ad un tratto le forze.　[12] svenuta.

[1], [12] What part of the verb is here substituted for the active participle? Why? [3] What did quasi mean in Ex. 2.? And here? What is the point of contact between the two meanings? [8] What verb is the root of affaccendati? [Fare, facendo.] [9] Avanzi is from the verb —? What does it mean? Point out the connexion between the two meanings.

---

5. THE MOTHER INSEPARABLE FROM THE DAUGHTER.

Elizabeth Eberts married, the day 3rd April of the year 1780, Henry Gabel grenadier in the royal regiment Deux-Ponts, the eve of its embarkation for America. The 20th March of 1781 this woman gave to the light a daughter at Rhode Island, and the following May the regiment departed from there for the expedition of York Town in Virginia.

In this long and painful march, Elizabeth carried her baby now between the arms and now on the shoulders with such *inconvenience*¹ that several Americans *flocked*² to see the French troops, piteous of her lot, offered themselves to deliver her from that hindrance by making acquisition of the girl. Every one can believe that she refused constantly such proposals, and that sometimes she replied to the offerers with those words which do not surprise in mouth of the wife of a grenadier.

The regiment at last arrived at Harford, capital of the province of Connecticut, where the army *mustered*³ and sojourned some time. Several families made anew to Elizabeth the same offer, some proposing to that poor woman, in payment of the baby, even to two hundred piastres; "Leave me in peace," she answered them, "I would not give her you for all your America."

Finally husband and wife, two rich citizens of Harford who were without offspring and without hope of having any, proposed to Elizabeth to adopt her daughter and to insure her fortune in the most strict legal *forms*⁴. The offer was in truth seductive, and if the mother had been able to separate her own happiness from that of the daughter, this time she would have bent herself to abandon her, but her heart could not endure such a *severance*[5], and she loved better to carry with her the daughter, as she had done from Rhode Island into Virginia, so from Virginia to Boston, that is nothing less than for a tract of road six hundred and fifty leagues long.

The French generals and the commanders of the regiment Deux-Ponts, witnesses of this fact and taken with admiration for a mother of such character, made her a present of twentyfive louis.

[1] disagio. [2] accorsi. [3] si raccolse. [4] modi. [5] disgiugnimento.

[1] Disagio is literally *discomfort* or *hardship*. [4] Modi, literally *modes* or *ways*.

---

6. At what Price a Son may be saved [1].

A lady of quality was returning into France from Martinique with a baby. At small distance from the port they were *overtaken*[2] by a violent storm. There was not in the vessel *who*[3] did not lend himself to the work; but the efforts *turned out*[4] useless. The consternation spread itself through the crew and through the passengers; the ship absorbed the water at every *point*[5]; the danger grew, and hope was vanishing; few moments were wanting to the sinking. The death presenting itself with all its horror, the greater number, amid the sobs and the *cries*[6] of despair, threw itself into the sea, and perished where it hoped still to find safety.

A Negro, who *attended* [*served*] the lady, embraces the son, *bids*[7] the mother hold on to a *skirt*[8] of his garment, and thus springs into the waves. In spite of the excessive hindrance, he swims with a courage that has not limits, and redoubles the exertion in proportion as the fatigue *would overcome him*[9]. But the *miserable* [*desolate*] mother perceives that *his strength is* [*the strengths go*] failing him; she expresses to him her *alarm* [*palpitations*]; the Negro *would wish*[10] to inspire in her courage; she is at last convinced that it is not possible to him to save two persons: "Save me the son," cries the unfortunate, "think no more of me; tell him only, if thou save him, that his mother died for him." This said, she detaches herself from the Negro who would wish still to hold her; the son is safe, but the mother dies for his love.

Nature is fertile of these examples *by which to give the lie to*[11] that philosophy which ascribes *all our virtues* [*every our virtue*] to the mere personal interest.

---

[1] si salvi (pres. subj.).   [2] côlti (part. of cogliere).   [3] chi.   [4] riuscirono.   [5] parte.   [6] urli.   [7] impone a.   [8] lembo.   [9] vorrebbe domarlo.   [10] vorrebbe.   [11] onde smentire.

[3] What is chi here? [An indef. substantive pronoun.] Give an example of the same use of *who*. ["Who steals my purse steals trash."]   [6] What is urli literally? [Howls.]   [7] Imporre is *to impose;* point out the primary meaning, and the connexion between the two meanings.   [9] Why not the conditional of domare? [Because the idea is not that under certain conditions he would be overcome, but that fatigue, here personified, is trying to overcome him.]

7. The Son of Metellus to liberate his Father offers his own life.

A few days[1] after the celebrated battle of Actium Octavianus Augustus was passing in review the prisoners of war. Metellus, one of the most cruel enemies who had been against him, was in their number. Although the *irritation*[2], the *hardship*[3], the hunger had disfigured him, nevertheless his son, who was serving in the army of Augustus, recognized him: ran to him, and under the eyes of all threw himself between his arms. After having kissed him, kissed him again and inundated him all with tears, holding him thus clasped, he turned the eyes and the ardent face to Augustus: "Yes," he said, "my father was your enemy; as such *he must*[4] die; but reflect however that I have served you with fidelity, that I have exposed the life for you: I deserve a recompense. I demand of you one only thing; for pity's sake save my father, and give to me in his stead the death." That attitude, these words expressed with the tongue of affection, moved to pity Augustus, who in that same moment granted the pardon to Metellus in recompense of the filial piety.

[1] Qualche giorno. [2] dispetto. [3] stento. [4] deve.

[1] Why is giorno in the singular? [Because no noun following qualche is capable of the plural form, though it may be understood in the plural sense.] [2] Dispetto is of course the same as the French *dépit*, and the old English *despite;* no word in familiar use now is its exact equivalent. [3] Stento, from the same root as the verb stentare, implies effort as well as hardship; egli stentava a vivere, he had hard work to live. [4] What does deve imply here?

8. THE DESERTER THROUGH FILIAL LOVE.

After the victory of Marseilles, whilst the Marshal Catinat was *surrounded* [*girded*] by the commanders who were congratulating *him* [*themselves with him*][1], an old soldier of his regiment breaks the *crowd*[2] and throws himself at his feet. "My general," he says, "I come in name of all the troop to beg of you *pardon* [*grace*] for a valiant soldier, discovered as a deserter, but who today however has taken a banner from the enemy and has made several prisoners." The marshal raising him with kindness, "Let us see him," said he, "this valorous deserter; guide him hither."

He was not far off. Introduced into the circle and *kneeling*[3] at the feet of the marshal, he spoke to him in this form. "My father, I am a *gentleman*[4], born of an officer who remained killed in the battle of Lens. My mother, without goods of fortune and without protectors, was obliged to work indefatigably to live and to maintain me, but *she having become*[5] helpless and reduced to extreme misery, I made myself a soldier to procure her a subsistence. I heard soon after that she was dangerously ill; I asked the leave to go to succour her, and it *was* [*came*] not granted me. Not being able to resist the imperious sentiments of nature, I have deserted and ran to assist her. But when I saw her *recovered* [*re-established*], I returned spontaneously to my *colours* [*banners*]. Yesterday, I endeavoured to cancel the shame of my crime. I know nevertheless that I deserve to die. I implore not *pardon* [*grace*] for myself. I ask only that when I shall be dead, you, my good general, *may take* [*may have*] care of my poor mother. . . . "

3

"My son," answered the marshal raising him, "why didst thou not come to find me before disobeying the law? If thou thoughtest me a barbarian, why now *then*[6] gavest thou me the name of father? Thy birth, and better still thy sentiments suffer not that thou be a *common* [*simple*] soldier; henceforward thou shall be officer; thy mother shall *be* [*come*] assisted, and I will recompense thy good comrade who *has served thee as*[7] introducer. Go; the King shall be informed of all; remember to be always a worthy gentleman, as thou art an excellent son."

Catinat procured a pension *for* [*to*] this unhappy mother; and because he could not immediately obtain it, he made it *be paid* [*pay*][8], in name of the king, with his own money, in order not to injure the delicacy of the given word.

[1]secolui. [2]calca. [3]genuflesso. [4]gentiluomo. [5]essendo ella divenuta. [6]poi. [7]ti ha fatto da.

[2]Calca is literally *press*. [3]What part of the verb is genuflesso? Why is it used here? (See Ex. 3, note 2.) [4]Gentiluomo is the *definite* term for *gentleman* (as if he had said "I am of gentle blood"); it contrasts with plebeo. [5]Why does the gerund here precede its nominative? You cannot know, for the rule is not usually given in grammars, though Italians instinctively observe it: — Because the nominative of the gerund is not the same as that of the principal verb; if it were, its place might be either before or after the gerund. Ex. Il padre passeggiando (*or* passeggiando il padre) nel giardino, incontrò il figlio: here padre is nom. to both verbs, therefore its place is free. But — Passeggiando il padre, il figlio lo raggiunse: here padre is nom. to the gerund *only*, therefore follows it; the nom. to raggiunse is figlio. — Can the nominative to the gerund be left out when it is a pronoun, as here in the exercise? Only when it is nominative also to the principal verb, which is not here the case. [6]Parse these four words. Why is da the right preposition? Because it expresses fitness or adap-

tation; agì da galantuomo, he acted like a man of honour; legna da bruciare, wood fit to burn. [6]Is not this substitution of the active for the passive infinitive contrary to the genius of the language? Not here, the rule being the same as in French; viz. that *fare* always governs the infinitive in the active form, though it may convey a passive sense.

---

9. The loving Daughter.

Gustavus III, king of Sweden, was traversing alone on horseback a village little distant from the capital. *He met [met himself in]*[1] a young and beautiful peasant-girl, who was drawing water at a fountain; he asked of her to drink, and the girl presented him at once the pail with those spontaneous graces *with*[2] which nature *uses to*[3] beautify her best productions. *Thereby*[4] remained struck the monarch, and said to her: "Beautiful maid, if you will follow me to Stockholm I will make your fortune." — "Sir," she answered, *"if [when]* even I ought to lend faith to your words, it would be to me impossible to profit by them. My mother is poor and infirm; she has not other support than me, and no thing of the world could make me renounce to assist her." — "Where is this your mother?" resumed the monarch. — "In that cottage, O sir, which you see there." — Gustavus *alighted [descended to ground]*, and followed the girl, entering with her into the hut.

What spectacle to eyes not accustomed to see the suffering humanity! *There met his eyes [To him showed itself]* a dirty little bed, on which was lying a miserable old woman, all *drawn together [contracted]*, who could not move a finger without *uttering [putting]* a

3 *

groan. "Ah! poor woman," exclaimed the prince *appalled*[5],
"how much are you worthy of compassion!" — "And I
should be *so* [*it*] much more," answered him the *sick
woman* [*infirm*], "without that good daughter who with
the most assiduous cares endeavours to alleviate my
ills: "God bless me her."

Her tears provoked those of the King, who laid a
purse on the bed. "Continue," he said to the daughter,
"Continue to console this unhappy one: it will be my
thought to *remove*[6] the want from this house. Your
virtues render you worthy to have *as a* [*in*] husband
the *best man* [*man most honest*] of the kingdom: I am
Gustavus."

He went out without awaiting answer, and having
returned to Stockholm, assigned, the day after, to the
mother a *life pension, lapsing afterwards to the*[7] daughter.

[1] s'incontrò in. [2] di. [3] suole. [4] ne. [5] sbigottito. [6] allontanare.
[7] pensione vitalizia, ricadente poi nella.

[3] Give the infin. of this verb. [6] Give the adj. from which
this verb is derived.

10. The Fast through filial Love.

A *lad, pupil*[1] of a French military school, would
not eat except a soup and little bread a day, nor drank
he but water. The *master* [*regent*] advertised of this
singularity, attributed it to an excess of ill-understood
devotion, and chid him for it: but the youth *still*[2] continued to live as before. The master *conveyed* [*passed*]
the information of it to the head of the administration,

who *having-caused to be conducted to him* [*made to
himself conduct*] the pupil, admonished him that *it was
absolutely requisite*[3] to conform himself to the discipline of the college, and sought to know the motive of
his singular conduct. The youth refusing to give him
a satisfactory answer, the superior *began* [*made himself*]
to menace him that *he would have turned him out*[4] of
house if he had not clearly explained himself on this
article.

Such menace made much impression on his spirit,
and determined him to manifest that which with so
much jealousy he was hiding. "In house of my father, O sir," he said, "there was not eaten but bread
bad and in small quantity; here, on the contrary, one
lives very well. *I have to the utmost endeavoured*[5] to
profit by it; but when I place myself at table, I cannot any more swallow a mouthful because *there comes
to my mind*[6] the state in which I left my father and
my mother, and the *straits*[7] in the which only too
much also at the present they *must* [*shall*] find themselves."

This account vividly moved the administrator.
"Since your father has served," said he, "*he will
draw*[8] at least some pension." — "No, sir," answered
the lad; "he was long at Versailles to obtain it, but
the want of money has since constrained him to abandon the project." — "*And well*"[9], returned the other,
"if the fact is certain as appears on your lip, *I will
get for him*[10] a pension. Since however, from how
much I understand, your parents will not have been
able to *furnish* [*accompany*] you with *any*[11] money,
accept these three louis which I give you in name of
the king, and it shall be my care, in few days, to

make *reach*[12] your father the first six months *in advance* [*anticipated*] of that pension which he will obtain by my means." — "But, sir," resumed the lad, "in what way will you be able to make reach him this money?" — "Let me do," answered the administrator, *well shall I know*[13] to find the road." — "Ah! since you have so much facility," resumed the good boy, "do me the great pleasure to remit to him also the three louis which you *made me a present of*[14]; here they would be useless to me, and my poor father will know well how to employ them *to the support*[15] of my brothers."

[1]fanciullo, alunno.   [2]tuttavia.   [3]conveniva assolutamente. [4]lo avrebbe cacciato.   [5]mi sono possibilmente sforzato.   [6]mi risovviene.   [7]angustie.   [8]riscuoterà.   [9]Ebbene.   [10]gli farò ottenere io. [11]qualche.   [12]giungere a.   [13]saprò ben io.   [14]mi regalaste.   [15]a sostegno.

[3]The proper meaning of *convenire* is *to be suitable* or *becoming*; it nearly corresponds to the English *to behove*, and exactly to the Biblical use of the expression *to be convenient*. Shew the connection between the two meanings of *convenient*.   [4]Of course the idiomatic English here would be, "he would turn him out." But this use, in Italian, of the past conditional is correct when the rest of the verbs (as si fece here) are in a past tense. A second instance occurs in this very sentence, and it will meet you continually in these exercises.   [5]Possa = potere; possibilmente = a tutto potere = to the utmost of my power.   [10]Parse these four words, and say why io comes last.   [14]Regalo = present: regalare = to make a present.

11. The beneficent Surprise.

The day after our departure from Glasgow, said an Englishman who has published 'his travels, we were constrained to stop at a little town, near to Lanark. Not knowing what to do, we were *lounging* [*thrown*] at a window of the inn, opposite to the prisons, observing those who passed. We saw *appear*[1] a man on horseback, dressed *in* [*of*] white cloth; he stopped at our inn, descended to earth and consigned to the host the horse.

This done, he regarded with surprise a poor old man, occupied in sweeping the street; drew near to him, and having-saluted him politely, took the broom from his hand and set himself to sweep *in his stead*[2], saying: "*At* [*in the*] your age, this is *over labour*[3] for you, dear old man. Have you not perhaps sons who can relieve you?" — "*Rather*[4] I have of them three," answered that man, "but what matters it? no one is *in a condition* [*in grade*] to lend me assistance." — "And why this?" added the stranger. — "Because the firstborn is in the East Indies, where he has obtained the grade of captain; the second made himself he also soldier with the *flattering hope*[5] of meeting the same fortune; and the third, poor boy! has answered for me. *He has taken on himself*[6] my debts, has not been able to pay them, and is in prison for my cause." — This said, he *began* [*set himself*] to weep.

The traveller returned the broom, turned himself back for an instant, and hid between his hands his face. Then having-turned himself to the old man, with air somewhat *frowning*:[7] "This your firstborn," he said, "this unnatural son, who yet is captain, has he not ever had heart to send you some succour to draw you from indigence?" — "Pray! speak not thus," interrupted him the good man: "my son is worthy person, he loves and respects his father, he has sent me money and not little, but I had the misfortune to lose it all, making myself surety for a *worthy man*[8] whom a series of adversities has rendered powerless to pay, and who has thus occasioned my ruin."

Then a youth, *projecting*[9] his head from the grating of the prison, set himself to cry out: "My father, if William lives, see him there; he is that one who speaks with you." — "*That is* [*It goes*] well, dear brother," answered the traveller, "thou hast recognised me at once;" and this saying, he rushed between the arms of the old man who *was on the point of falling swooning*[10] from the excess of the jubilation.

When a little old woman, who stood at the door of a hovel, at little distance, *comes* [*makes herself*] forward exclaiming: "Ah! where is my dear William? come, my son, come to embrace thy mother." Scarcely the captain saw her, he detached himself from the paternal arms, he precipitated into hers.

We are descended at that point, and have increased the number of the spectators flocked from all the corners to this scene most *affecting* [*penetrating*]. Mr. Blamble, who was with me at the balcony, *passing through*[11] the crowd, drew near to the traveller and said to him: "Captain, we are here *putting up at* [*of passage in*] the inn, and would have *gone* [*done*] willingly a hundred leagues to be present at this tender meeting with your fortunate family; do us a great pleasure, unite yourselves all and come to dinner with us." The officer *received politely*[12] the invitation; he added however that he would not have placed himself at table, *if* [*when*] first he had not replaced in liberty his brother, with whom he *wanted* [*willed*] to dine even from the first day. In fact the prisoner came out, at the end of one hour, the captain having deposited the sum for which he was held in arrest. All the family came then to our inn, and every one lavished caresses on the excellent William, who corresponded to all with fulness of heart.

Mr. Brown, for thus was called this officer, as soon as freely he could converse with us, held to us this discourse: "Sirs, today *only*[13] I taste in all their extent the favours of the fortune. My uncle made me learn the trade of weaver, but I corresponded ill to his attentions, and disdaining the domestic discipline, enrolled myself in the troops of the *East India Company* [*Company of the Indies*]. The exactness with which I have served my lord Clive has gained me his kindness; I ascended *from* [*of*] grade to grade, became captain, and the chest of the regiment was entrusted to me. I made myself steward; I was on the occasion merchant; and when *I attained*[14] to secure myself a fund of twenty thousand pounds sterling, I renounced the *military life*[15]. To say the truth, I have not *neglected*[16] to send three times money to my father; but the first sum of two hundred pounds sterling is the only one that has reached him; the second fell into the hands of a *bankrupt*[17], and I entrusted the third to a Scotch gentleman who died on the voyage; I hope however that the heirs will return it to me."

He manifested to us *afterwards*[18] his intentions, and they were to disburse at once to his father fifty pounds sterling, *to the end that*[19] they might provide

for his most pressing wants; to assign eighty by the
year to both his parents, transferable afterwards, after
their death, to the brothers; to buy a *commission* [20] *for*
[*to*] the second, and to collocate the third in quality
of director and of partner in a manufactory which it
was proposed to establish; to *give* [*make a present of*]
five hundred pounds sterling to a sister married *to* [*in*]
a farmer of scanty fortunes, to distribute of them fifty
to the poor, and to give a most brilliant *entertainment*
[*feast*] to his compatriots.

[1]comparire. [2]in sua vece. [3]soverchia fatica. [4]anzi. [5]lusinga.
[6]si e accollato. [7]accigliata. [8]galantuomo. [9]sporgendo. [10]fu
per cadere tramortito. [11]trapassando. [12]accolse gentilmente. [13]sol-
tanto. [14]giunsi. [15]milizia. [16]trascurato. [17]fallito. [18]quindi.
[19]affinchè. [20]carica.

[3]Fatica, labour; faticare, to labour. *Fatigue* is scarcely ever
a correct translation of this word. [4]Anzi is one of the most idiomatic conjunctions; it strengthens the idea by apparently negati-
ving it. [6]Accollarsi = mettersi intorno al collo. [10]Essere per =
to be on the point of; one of the ways of translating the French
aller when it denotes an immediate future. "Il va partir = è per
partire = he is going to set off." — Why is cadere in the infinitive? Is tramortito a participle? No, an adjective; though there
is the neuter verb tramortire to faint. [13]Often a far more idiomatic form than solo. Soltanto = sol tanto = only so much.
[16]A more idiomatic and familiar verb than negligere. Trascurato
(cura is the root) = careless or heedless; an adjective in constant
use. "Che ragazzo trascurato! what a careless boy!"

12. Eudocia Empress.

Eudocia Athenian, who before the baptism was called Athenais, daughter of the philosopher Heraclitus, possessed the graces of her sex and the firmness of ours. She had *as* [*in*] master in the letters and in the sciences her father, who made of this daughter a philosopher, a *grammarian*,[1] a *rhetorician*[2]. The good old man thought that so many *advantages* [*prerogatives*], coupled with so much beauty, ought to suffice her to form her fortune, and deprived her of the inheritance. She thinking otherwise, chose, after his death, to *insist on* [*make avail*] the rights which nature and the laws gave her, and found in the brothers, as indeed uses to happen, the most dogged and indomitable resistance.

Eudocia had the soul too intrepid to cede her rights. She *determined* [*deliberated*] nothing less than to *betake herself*[3] to Constantinople, and to *plead her own*[4] cause in face of Pulcheria, sister of Theodosius II, a man so indolent that he left in *her full keeping*[5] his person and his empire.

The project executed, Pulcheria remained highly surprised at the spirit, at the learning, at the *charms*[6] of this Greek. She was *so*[7] taken by them that she *determined* [*deliberated*] to make her wife to Theodosius, and thus to have her as sister-in-law; and the affair *was* [*came*] on the instant by reciprocal consent concluded, as would be done on a stage.

What *amazement*[8] and fear in the brothers of Eudocia when they heard these nuptials! But she, who had the soul worthy of the throne, invited them courteously to betake themselves to the palace, and not so

soon[9] did she see them, than drawing a veil over the
past, she announced to them, with the fraternal affection
on the lip, that she had nominated them to the first
dignities of the empire.

[1] grammatico. [2] retore. [3] recarsi. [4] perorare la propria. [5] piena
di lei balia. [6] avvenenza. [7] talmente. [8] sbigottimento. [9] tosto.

---

13. The Swimmer.

In the year 1585, a vessel *wrecked*[1] laden with
Portuguese troops who were voyaging to the Indies.
The crew attempted to save itself on two *skiffs*[2], one
of which landed happily at the lands of the Kaffirs,
but the pilot of the other warned the Captain Edward
Mello, that the danger was extreme of sinking, *if* [*when*]
there were not thrown into sea a dozen of victims.

The *lot*[3] amongst the others fell upon a soldier
who had with him a younger brother. It was this
youth who begged to be cast into water instead of the
other: "He is much more clever," he went saying,
"and more industrious than I; he can maintain my
father, my mother and my sisters, whilst I should be
incapable of it; if they should lose him, they would
be exposed to die of hunger; *you preserve*[4] their life
saving his, whilst mine would be to them of little advantage."

The captain accepted such reasons, and the youth
jumped into the sea, but when he was there, the love
of the preservation made itself *felt* [*feel*] with all its
impetuosity, and infused an extraordinary strength into
this heroic soldier, who followed, swimming, the boat

for six continuous hours, in the unceasing hope to be able to grasp it. He reached it at last, *clutched*[5] it and made the last efforts to introduce himself there-into, although with the swords *drawn*[6] it was threatened to kill him. His firmness, his miserable state, and more still the remembrance of the generous action which he had performed, move to pity the *sailors:*[7] they grant that he may re-enter, and he saves the brother and himself.

[1] naufragò. [2] palischermi. [3] sorte. [4] conservate. [5] abbrancò. [6] sguainate. [7] naviganti.

[1] A neuter instead of a passive verb; not an uncommon idiom. [5] Abbrancare, literally to seize with *branche*, claws. [6] Guaina = sheath: therefore sguainato = unsheathed.

14. The Heroic Substitution.

Some English slaves in Algiers *were awaiting*[1] from day to day their liberation. One of these, by name Williams, by profession a soldier, was at first *subjected* [*submitted*] to *a very hard*[2] life; but in progress his lot *softened itself*[3], and there *was* [*came*] to him every day granted some hour of liberty. He frequenting the baths found again there by chance an elder brother of his who *had been* [*was*][4] a slave *since*[5] twelve years, and whom he supposed already dead, but so disfigured by hardships and by labours that he had no little difficulty to know him. This unexpected and loving *encounter*[6] *was* [*came*] followed by frequent *interviews*[7], until the time arrived in which Williams could restore himself to the *native-country*[8]. Constrained to abandon a brother in a situation very deplorable, he embraced the heroic *resolve*[9] to remain slave in his stead: "You are," he said to him, "extremely weakened, whilst I am healthy and robust; *I charge myself willingly with that load*[10] under which you would succumb. If it shall please God to *grant* [*concede*] you the *means*[11] to liberate me, I am certain that you will not fail at once to profit thereby." After long resistance, the brother accepted the offer, and the master without opposition *agreed* [*adhered*] to an exchange which *would prove to him*[12] most useful.

[1]attendevano.' [2]penosissima. [3]si raddolcì. [5]da. [6]incontro. [7]abboccamenti. [8]patria. [9]partito. [10]mi carico volentieri quel peso. [11]mezzo. [12]gli riusciva.

[4]Era stato would be right if he had ceased to be a slave at the time to which the verb refers. [7]What noun is the root of abboccamenti? Bocca. [10]Caricare governs the reflective pronoun in the dative case, and the thing carried in the accusative. [11]Mezzo = means: commonly used in the singular, like the Fr. *moyen*. [12]The conditional tense expresses no contingency here, and is therefore rendered by the imperfect. — Riuscire is strictly *to turn out;* but this would imply that the issue was not certain beforehand, whereas the reverse was here the case.

---

15. The loving Division of the Goods.

M. de Pastoret of Marseilles kept two brothers as *farmers*[1] in an *estate*[2] of his, who were bound together by the most lively love. Both took wife and lived in community of goods, and sufficiently tranquilly, for a

notable length of time. But the women who belonged
to other families, and who had opposed interests, *were
no longer able* [*knew not more*] to agree between
themselves; *in the which*[3] there is nothing of surprising. The wife of the firstborn was of a difficult
temper, and in nine years of marriage was become
mother of ten children; the other was barren, and
knew perhaps too well some her personal advantages.
A very great quarrel[4] *sprang up* [*was born*] *one day*[5]
between the sisters-in-law, and the quarrels in Provence
resemble the *storms*[6] of the climate. It was deliberated
to come to the division: the women *would have it*[7],
and *it must needs be* [*needed well*] that the husbands
should consent to it.

In similar circumstances *custom*[8] *requires* [*brings*]
that the one of the two makes the portions, and the
other chooses that which most *he likes* [*pleases him*].
The partition was made by the firstborn, and the day
came *on* [*in*] which, for the choice, *they both convoked
themselves*[9] with the wives and with the children. The
silence, the pallor, some tear that *watered*[10] the cheeks,
manifested what was the state of their hearts. The
younger laid at last the hand on one of the two parts:
"I choose this, O brother," said he; "but, *mind well*[11],
that it is not just." — "Thou *art mistaken* [*deceivest
thyself*]," rejoined the firstborn; "assure thyself that it
is; and besides, thou well knowest that I am exact."
— "I know it, but these two parts are not equal; in
that which I choose the best is wanting. Thinkest
thou, cruel, that I, without children, *will*[12] divide the
goods and not divide likewise she family? I also *want*[13]
the half of it; I want five of thy children, and give
me the smallest, because the biggest can be to thee

useful. My wife thinks, she also, thus ...." The novelty of the *affectionate*[14] project, the *quivering*[15] of the voice, the sentiment of the expression *so*[16] struck all that *sad assemblage*[17], that it changed itself *in twinkling of eye*[18] into a delicious scene of love. The sisters ran to each other's neck, the children *began* [*set themselves*] to weep, and the brothers. . . . .

[1]fittaiuoli. [2]podere. [3]nel che. [4], [5]rissa fortissima. The order of this sentence is, Sprang up one day very great quarrel. [6]temporali. [7]la voleano. [8]consuetudine. [9]si convocarono entrambi. [10]irrigava. [11]avverti bene. [12]voglia. [13]voglio. [14]affettuoso. [15]tremito. [16]talmente. [17]mesta adunanza. [18]a colpo d'occhio.

[3]When the antecedent is a sentence or clause, the relative takes an article before it. [9]This must be here understood as a reflected, not a passive verb; the sense is, "they came together." [11]Avvertire, here a neuter verb, is active when it means *to warn.* [12]*Will* is not here the auxiliary of the future, but expresses a present volition. [14]Affettuoso is usually said of things, affezionato of persons. The same distinction holds good in French between *affectueux* and *affectionné*. [16]*So,* meaning *to such a degree,* is best rendered by talmente. [17]Adunanza has for its root uno; various individuals collected into *one* body.

---

16. The Admiral Chabot.

Francis I, King of France, reproved *the Admiral Chabot for* [*to the A. C.*] the friendly bonds which bound him to the Constable de Montmorency, fallen into disgrace and abandoned by all. "I prohibit you," the monarch said to him, "to have the least communication with him." This *prohibition*[1] was taken by Chabot as an *outrage*[2], and in that point reviving

themselves in him the tender sentiments which he
nourished towards *his* [*the*] friend: "Sire," he answered,
"I know of what I am debtor to my King, but I
forget not also the duties which friendship imposes on
me; *moreover*[3] the *Constable*[4] is a good subject, and
has served always well the State." This open answer
displeased the monarch, and he threatened the admiral
to subject him to a trial. "You can do it, O sire,"
resumed Chabot; "on this article I implore neither
grace, nor *delay*[5]; I have not a thing to reproach myself with; my life, my honour *have nothing* [*have not
of what*] to fear."

The King, yet more angered by this frank speaking,
ordered that he should be arrested and *confined*[6] in
the castle of Melun. *Then*[7] he charged the chancellor
Poyet that he should assemble a commission drawn
from the members of the Parliaments, *which was to
try*[8] that disgraced one.

The chancellor served with all the fervour the injustice of his *master*[9] He found easily the judges;
but the great difficulty was to find the crimes. Nevertheless, *by dint*[10] of *twisted*[11] interpretations to words
and to *deeds*[12] which yet had the impress of innocence,
they *succeeded* [*came to head*], not *indeed*[13] to prove,
but to make appear Chabot guilty, and as such was
pronounced against him the sentence of death.

Poyet was applauding himself to have succeeded in
this masterpiece of iniquity, and *joyous*[14] presented to
the King trial and sentence. The monarch, a man
susceptible of a transport, but yet incapable of con-
summating *in* [*at*] cold blood so much *wickedness*[15],
turned[16] the *indignant*[17] eyes from those papers, and
restoring his grace to Chabot, said frowning to the

chancellor: "I should not ever have believed that in my kingdom *there were* [*were found*][18] so many iniquitous judges."

[1] divieto. [2] ingiuria. [3] d'altronde. [4] contestabile. [5] dilazione. [6] chiuso. [7] quindi. [8] la quale dovesse formare il processo a. [9] padrone. [10] a forza. [11] contorte. [12] fatti. [13] già. [14] giulivo. [15] scelleratezza. [16] torso. [17] sdegnosi. [18] si fossero ritrovati.

[6] To confine = to shut up = chiudere. — Confinare must never be used in this sense; it is the term for the mediæval practice of assigning to dangerous persons certain limits (confini) within which they were free, but which they must not transgress. [8] Why la quale rather than che? Che would here be ambiguous, its grammatical antecedent being parlamenti; la quale can only refer to commissione. — [9] Padrone = master = owner or ruler. Maestro = master = instructor. [13] Già as an expletive somewhat corresponds to *of course*; but is often untranslatable, the tone of voice being the equivalent in English. It has something of the force of the German doch. Già s'intende = yes, of course. [16] The literal meaning? [17] Sdegnosi, adj.: sdegnati, part. Why is the former preferred here? Because it describes the state of a noun, not the *process* by which this state was attained. Be very attentive to this distinction; it is frequently important. It is akin to that between the use of werden and sein with the pass. part. in German.

17. The little Baker of Nérac.

The eve of the battle of Arques, the great Henry IV heard a young officer who was speaking the Gascon dialect, the first *language*[1] learnt by the King. He commanded him to *approach*[2]: "Of which country are you?" interrogated him the monarch. — "Sire," answered the youth, "you have often eaten the bread

of my father.." — "I! where ever?" — "At Nérac,
sire, where my father continues still to *carry on the
business of a [make the]* baker." — "Bravo, my comrade; this *shews you not [is not]* to want for wit.
How long have you been [From what time are you]
an officer?" — "[*From*] four days, sire. The lord de
la Tour d'Auvergne *promoted [did grace to]* me, instead of *promoting [doing it to]* my friend Classac who
merited it *more*[3]; but this depends because he knows
him not enough." — "Oh the fine words'" exclaimed
the King; „and I make officer thy friend Classac,
without knowing him, and will have particular care of
thee and of thy father baker."

[1]linguaggio. [2]appressarsi. [3]di più.

[1] Lingua = tongue = language (Fr. *langue*). Linguaggio
(Fr. *langage*) = language when not synonymous with *tongue*. Of
course linguaggio is a more restricted term, applicable, as here, to
a dialect; or to the use of words by a particular writer, or on a
particular occasion. — "Bello è qui il linguaggio del nostro autore
= this is a fine passage of our author. Perchè mi tenete un tal
linguaggio? why do you use such language to me?"

18. THE FEIGNED CONDEMNATION.

The lord of Châteauneuf, the year 1633, *was [came]*
arrested and conducted to the castle of Angoulême,
where the cardinal of Richelieu *wanted [willed]*[1] to subject him to an action. The adherents and the friends
were involved in the same *mishap*[2] and shut up in the
prisons of the Bastille. The object of this severe conduct was to induce them to depose against the arrested.

The chevalier Jars, *through*[3] inclination and through gratitude his intimate confidant and friend, was he *whose depositions were principally counted on*[4], inasmuch as, being poor, he was supposed the most exposed of all to seduction.

Resting on[5] such infamous principles, the cardinal minister attempted to bend him to his intentions with the most *alluring*[6] promises, which made not any effect on *his*[7] spirit. He changed *his mode of attack* [*battery*] and *had recourse*[8] to the most atrocious threats, which were equally impotent to shake him: the chevalier opened not mouth if not to *eulogize*[9] the merit of his tender friend.

Richelieu, who was not accustomed to endure *oppositions*[10], nor to renounce projects of his invention, induced the judges to abuse [*of*] their ministry, persuading them that they *should pronounce*[11] against him sentence of death, and assuring them that his only design was that of intimidating him, whilst it *would be* [*would have been*] his care *to obtain for him pardon*[12] from the King, before that the sentence should be executed. Jars listened to the reading of this *romantic*[13] decree, which had he been another man *might have* [*could*][14] cost him his life through fright, with that intrepidity which *is inspired in* [*inspires to*][15] a great soul *by* the consciousness of being an innocent victim of the most *repulsive*[16] violence, and set off to the scaffold as he would have done to the nuptials.

Glad [*Content*] to encounter death in order not to betray the cause of justice and his friend, he ascended tranquilly the scaffold erected by despotism; the fatal bandage girt his eyes, and bent down over the *block*[17] he awaited in peace the *last* [*extreme*] blow, when

53

there is raised [raises itself] a voice which announces
to him *his pardon [the grace]*.

The great man descends from the scaffold, and one
of the judges who had lent themselves to this abomi-
nable *plot* [18] places himself at once at his side, and
sets himself [19] to exalt to the supposed *criminal* [20] the
adorable clemency of the King, the ineffable moderation
of the cardinal, and exhorts him that he resolve at
last, in sight of so many benefactions, to reveal the
black designs of the lord of Châteauneuf. "You are
mistaken, O sir," answers him the chevalier: "there
shall not be drawn any advantage from the terror that
it was *expected [pretended]* to inspire in me by the
spectacle of death. I repeat to you that the lord of
Châteauneuf is an honest man who has always served
faithfully his sovereign and his native-land, that nothing
is known to me against his honour; but if even he
had entrusted to me some secret which *you would be
pleased* [21] to hear, I assure you that there would not
be force in the world capable to *snatch* [22] it from my
mouth."

A so great virtue *gained* [23] in recompense the *imprisonment* [24] in the Bastille for as much time as *was
needed* [25] in order that the constancy of the chevalier
should weary the rage of his vile persecutor.

[1] lo volea sottoporre a processo. [2] disgrazia. [3] per. [4] su le cui
deposizioni si contava principalmente. [5] appoggiato a. [6] lusinghiere.
[7] di lui. [8] ricorse. [9] encomiare. [10] contrasti. [11] pronunziassero.
[12] impetrargli grazia. [13] romanzesco. [14] potea. [16] ributtante. [17] ceppo.
[18] intreccio. [19] si fa. [20] reo. [21] aggradiste. [22] strappare. [23] riporto.
[24] prigionia. [25] fu d'uopo.

[1] Processo = legal *proceeding* = trial. [2] Seldom *disgrace.*
[5] Literally *leaning against.* [7] Suo would be grammatically ambi-

guous; di lui is not so, as its antecedent is the oblique case.
[8]A more concise form than ebbe ricorso. [9]What noun is from
the same Greek root? [10]Contrasto is from the same roots as
contrastare = contra stare = to withstand = stand against
= resist. [11]Why in the imperf. subj. rather than the conditional? It relates to the past and is governed by persuadere.
Consult Mariotti's Grammar if you have forgotten. [12]Impetrare, to
obtain by prayer. [13]Not to be confounded with romantico, which
is a literary term opposed to classico. [14]Avrebbe potuto would
not be wrong; but potea is more idiomatic. [15]What? an active
verb substituted for a passive? Yes, because here it renders the
sentence more vigorous and concise. [18]Literally *web;* as we say
to weave a plot. [20]Criminale is a *prison.* [24]Prigionia = the *state*
of imprisonment.

19. DOCTOR FRIEND.

The Englishman Friend, celebrated physician *to* [*of*]
the Queen, being a member of the parliament, spoke
against the conduct of the ministry in tone of old Roman, and for this not common fervour the court became
his enemy. *They began by stirring up against him
tiresome embarrassments; and they continued in such
manner to weave the plot*[1], that the poor doctor was
constrained at last to take lodging in the Tower of
London.

Already were passed six months of this *unpleasant*
[*ungrateful*] sojourn, when the minister fell ill, and sent
for his physician, who was the illustrious Mead. There
could not present itself to this man a finer occasion
to *aid*[2] his friend Friend, nor let he it *escape from*[3]
his hand. He betook himself to the minister, made
the most minute *researches*[4] into the nature of the

illness, and after mature pondering concluded that, the method of treatment which he had proposed to himself faithfully executed, the sick man would to a certainty be cured, and that of this he gave in *pledge*[5] his own life. "Expect not however," *he added*[6], "O sir, that I should order you *even*[7] a cup of water, *if* [*when*] first Doctor Friend be not gone out free from the Tower."

The minister showed at first an extreme repugnance to *grant*[8] the request, and let elapse some days without caring for the physician. But fortunately the illness *became more and more* [*made itself always more*] serious; and that gentleman who reposed exclusively on the skill of Mead, thought prudently to change his mind, and made him know that he had already *forwarded*[9] the petition to the King in order that Doctor Friend should recover the liberty.

Not for this the *wary*[10] Mead *yielded*[11] to commence the treatment. He chose first to certify himself that his friend had been restored to his family, and when he was sure of it, he applied then *promptly*[12] his lights to advantage of the sick man, and with such success that *ere long* [*in short*] he obtained the cure of him. That same day on which Friend went out from the Tower, Mead went to visit him, but only to consign to him five thousand guineas which he had collected *treating*[13] in his stead the sick persons who were used to have recourse to him.

[1] si cominciò dal suscitargli contro fastidiosi imbarazzi, e si proseguì a talmente ordire la trama. [2] giovare a. [3] sfuggire di. [4] indagini. [5] cauzione. [6] soggiunse. [7] nemmeno. [8] esaudire. [9] innoltrato. [10] accorto. [11] si piegò. [12] tantosto. [13] medicando.

¹Parse all this. Si cominciò is literally what? Why is it pre-
ferred here? What does contro govern? Gli. And suscitare?
Imbarazzi. Give the most literal English equivalents of this and fastidiosi, and shew the shades of difference in meaning. ²One of the
most idiomatic verbs, meaning *to be of use to another in any way;*
to be translated according to the sense. It is the reverse of nuo-
cere. ⁵This is the ordinary term for *bail* or *security*. ⁶A more
usual word than aggiunse when it means that something was added
to a speech. ⁷This is used instead of ancora in negative phrases.
⁸This verb means *to grant a prayer* or *request*, not *to grant* in
any other sense. ¹⁰From what verb is this adj. derived? ¹²Exactly
the Fr. *aussitôt*. ¹³Literally *medicating*.

20. THE CONSTANT FRIEND.

When the Pontiff Ganganelli, whose portrait princes
ought to keep hanging at the bed, was *no more*
[*not other*] than a simple monk, he nourished much
friendship for a painter of moderate ability, but of
excellent character. *Ganganelli being-promoted [Promoted
Ganganelli]* to the *cardinalate*¹, the poor artist dared
no longer present himself, and suspended every correspondence. Not seeing him appear, Ganganelli
*donned*² all the apparatus of his new dignity, surprised
him with this pomp in his house, gave him a hundred
sweet rebukes on his abandonment, *urged [excited]*
him to frequent him, protesting to him that his door
would have been always open for him.

Elected Ganganelli *to the pontificate [in pontiff]*,
there was]came] presented to him, *according to the
custom*³, the *roll*⁴ of the *household officers*⁵, in which
he found also inserted one of the most renowned painters
of Italy. "All goes well," said the Pontiff, "except the

article of the painter. He who here *is* [*comes*] proposed to me, is without doubt excellent; but I am such a figure that an artist cannot much advantage his reputation *by doing my* [*by the doing me the*] portrait. *Besides*[6], this man is rich and can live comfortably without me; *whereas*[7] I know one of them, inferior *indeed*[8] in merit, but of scant fortunes, and, *what* [*that which*] matters more, much my friend: behold him whom I elect *as* [*in*] my first painter."

[1]cardinalato. [2]vestì. [3]giusta il costume. [4]ruolo. [5]impiegati domestici. [6]d'altronde. [7]laddove. [8]bensì.

[2]Vestire, a. v. to don. Vestirsi di, refl. v. to clothe oneself with. [4]Ruolo = roll = list; whence arruolare, arrolare, to enroll.

---

21. The Tribune Cœdicius.

In the first Punic war, the Carthaginian general had the *prudence*[1] to occupy rapidly the heights, in the act that the Roman army had *imprudently entangled*[2] itself in the corresponding tortuous depths. This army was lost without the generous sacrifice of a true friend of Rome. Cœdicius, who yet *was no more than*[3] a tribune of the people, ran to the tent of the consul, and made him observe all the danger of his situation. "There remains but one only *course*[4] to take," added the great man, "and it is that of making immediately march a body of five hundred soldiers, as if one would force the passage on one side. The enemy fearing that they may be followed by all the rest, will carry to that point a great part of his forces; our legionaries will remain overwhelmed by the number, but meanwhile you will be able to profit by this moment to throw yourself with all the army on the opposite side, to open for yourself the passage and to take a more advantageous position." — "*That is all* [*It goes*] very well," answered the consul; "but who will be the officer who *will choose to*⁵ charge himself with this enterprise, sure to perish with the others?" — "Elect me," resumed *eagerly*⁶ the tribune; "and let my loss assure your *safety*⁷ and that of Rome."

Penetrated with admiration for this hero, the Consul remains at first *in suspense*⁸, nor knows *how to resolve* [*to resolve himself*] to immolate to the native-land a citizen so precious; but the impossibility to save otherwise the army, induces him at last to this deplorable sacrifice. And lo Cœdicius who gathers five hundred soldiers, places himself at their head, marches against the enemy, *surrounds* [*invests*] him. The Carthaginians run *in*⁹ torrents and put *in*⁹ pieces this advanced body; but, by a species of prodigy, Cœdicius perishes not with them. He returns covered with wounds and with glory; the army of Rome is debtor to him *for* [*of*] its safety, he is so happy *as to recover*¹⁰, and continues to render by his valour signal services to his native-land.

¹accortezza. ²inavvedutamente impegnato. ³altro non era fuorchè. ⁴partito. ⁵vorrà. ⁶vivacemente. ⁷salvezza. ⁸sospeso. ⁹a. ¹⁰di risanare.

¹What verb is the root? [Accorgersi.] ²And what of inavvedutamente? ⁴Fr. *parti*. ⁷This word, unlike its synonym sicurtà, implies a previous danger. ⁸The literal meaning? ¹⁰Risanare,

here a neuter, is often an active verb; its root is of course sano.
— "Èrisanato il paziente; il medico l'ha risanato."

22. THE TAKING OF CALAIS.

In the year 1347, Edward III, King of England,
saw perish the flower of his troops under Calais, which
had *disappointed* [*deluded*] his efforts through the course
almost of a year. Irritated by *such* [*a such*] obstinate
resistance, he refused at first to accord to the inhabitants the *least*[1] favourable condition, resolved that all
should perish under the *sword*[2]; his generals however
having made him observe[3] that the French *would
avenge* [*would have avenged*] this *slaughter*[4] by the
massacre[5] of the prisoners fallen into their power, he
reduced his *claim* [*pretension*] to six victims who were
to present themselves to him with the head bare, with
the rope *round* [*to*] the neck and with the keys of
the city in hand.

Mauny was charged to *impart*[6] to the inhabitants
the last *will*[7] of the victor. The commandant of the
wretched[8] city, John de Vienne, prayed him to *stay*[9]
and to *be present* [*assist*] at the declaration which he
was about to make of it to the assembly of the people.
All gathered themselves in the square, agitated by the
uncertainty of living, or of dying. When there was
heard the resolution of the King, a deep silence announced the general consternation: some weep, some
groan, some seek in vain with their eyes these six
victims of the public safety. De Vienne, a warrior
so intrepid *at* [*on*] the breach, *mingles* [*confounds he*]

also his palpitations with those of the desolate fellow-citizens, and *even Mauny himself*[10], witness of [*a*] such spectacle, cannot withhold his tears.

But the time passes; his master expects him, he cannot wait any longer. When behold Eustace de Saint-Pierre rise up intrepid among that crowd of lost folk, and kindled *by* [*of*] a noble ardour *break forth*[11] into these accents: "Sirs, *as many as you are here*[12], great sin it would be to let perish an entire people and a people like this, whilst I suppose that whoever *would*[13] save it from the *extermination*[14] would find much grace with the Most High. I hold so strong hope to *obtain*[15] pardon, if I die for this people, that *I will*[16] be the first."

Such words *transported the bystanders from*[17] themselves, and received the *recompense* [*retribution*] most flattering that a feeling soul can promise itself: one prostrated himself at his feet, another clasped his knees, another kissed his hands, another bathed him with tears: *in his presence was*[18] every one in act of adoration. John d'Aire, jealous of the glory of his cousin, *cleaves*[19] also he the crowd, places himself at the side of Eustace, and *declares his desire to share* [*protests to will to divide*] with him the honour of this death; and behold James and Peter Wisant, loving brothers, *approach*[20] they also, and imitating the same heroic resolution, *show themselves*[20] worthy relations of the first. Ah! why ever history, which has *handed down*[21] to us the names of so many illustrious *rogues*[22], has it then neglected to preserve to us those of the other two victims?

Then the venerable old man De Vienne, with the heart *pierced*[23], mounts on horseback and accompanies the heroes, followed by a crowd of tearful people, *as far as* [24] to the gate of the city, where arrived he consigns them to Mauny, and conjures him to interpose his mediation to obtain mercy to - these *brave men* [25], worthy of recompense *rather than* [26] of chastisement.

Arrived at the camp, and divulged the fame of their magnanimity, they *were* [*came*] dragged before the Monarch in the abject form prescribed, and *presented* [27] to him the keys of the city. At such spectacle there rose around the King a murmur mixed of amazement and of compassion; *Edward alone* [*the only Edward*] inflexible, cast a severe look on his victims, and opened not mouth except to say: "Be they at once beheaded."

Heard such words, the prince of Wales prostrated himself at the feet of his father, and made every effort *to move to pity* [28] his heart; he heard nothing but repulses, and the pitiless sentence: "Let the *executioner* [29] draw near immediately".

The illustrious unhappy ones were already about to bend the neck to the axe, and would have certainly perished, if there had not presented herself the queen herself, who had followed into France Edward. This estimable woman, grieved at the aspect of the inflexibility of her husband, and blushing for him, threw herself also she at his feet and supplicated him, in name of religion, of humanity, of honour, to triumph once over himself, not to *sully* [30] with this act of cruel baseness his victory, to open *in short* [31] his heart to generosity, to compassion, to pardon. — Edward appeared confused, cast down his eyes, was silent for few instants; *afterwards* [32], "I would like better," said he,

that you were elsewhere; one cannot resist you: do
with them that which pleases you."

The queen rises exultant, thanks the monarch, orders
the heroes to follow her, makes them be clothed de-
cently, *prepares for them a banquet*[33], *gives*[34] to each
six pieces of gold, and wills that they should *be [come]*
jealously escorted even to the gates of that city, which
they loved more than the life.

[1]menoma. [2]ferro. [3]avendogli fatto osservare. [4]eccidio.
[5]strage. [6]partecipare. [7]volontà. [8]sciagurata. [9]trattenersi. [10]per-
fino lo stesso **M.** [11]prorompere. [12]quanti qui siete. [13]volesse.
[14]esterminio. [15]conseguire. [16]voglio. [17]rapirono gli astanti a.
[18]al suo cospetto stava. [19]fende. [20]*In the infinitive.* [21]tramandato.
[22]furfanti. [23]trafitto. [24]sino. [25]prodi. [26]anzichè. [27]porsero.
[28]per impietosire. [29]carnefice. [30]deturpare. [31]in fine. [32]poscia.
[33]imbandisce loro un convito. [34]dona.

[1]A less usual form of minima. What part of speech is it?
[2]Poetical for spada. [3]Parse this. [6]Like our *to impart.* [8]A
word very exactly corresponding in use to *wretched:* not necessarily — not here, for example — implying wickedness, yet continually applied to wicked persons. [9]To stay for a time; to linger.
[18]Stare must be translated according to the sense; perhaps here
the closest rendering would be *held himself.* It always implies a
more or less settled posture or action, being a verb of station (that
is, not of *motion*). [20]The pres. indic. would not be wrong; but
the more concise and picturesque infin. is often a more idiomatic
form after ecco. [25]The Fr. *preux.* [29]A more noble term for boja.
[30]From *turpe* = morally defiled and base. [32]The Fr. *puis*; used
in giving an account of *successive* actions. [33]Imbandire is used
only of *preparing a meal.* — Convito always implies the *invitation*
of at least one guest; in this it differs from banchetto, which implies only the festive character of the meal. [34]From *dono*; — a
less general verb than dare.

23. THE LOVE OF COUNTRY RECOMPENSED.

Margaret of Valois, *being at war with* [*war moved to*][1] her brother and [*to*] her husband, had caused to be surrounded by her army Villeneuve d'Agenois, and fearing to expose herself to *very heavy*[2] losses, *if* [*when*] she should have been constrained to subject that city by force, ordered a *picquet*[3] of about forty soldiers to drag beneath the walls Charles de Cicutat, whom she had in her hands, and to *slay*[4] him, *in case that*[5] his son, who commanded the *fortress*[6], should have refused to open its gates. Charles, the intimation heard, in place of *discussing*[7] his own cause, cried aloud: "Remember, my son, thy duty: if *I incited thee*[8] to surrender, I should be no more thy father, but a traitor, an abject, an enemy of thine and of thy king."

Whilst he was pronouncing these words worthy of an ancient Roman, the guards had already lifted up the pikes upon his breast; when the young Cicutat made sign that they should suspend the blow. The gates *were* [*came*] opened, and he issued thence, accompanied by only four soldiers, as if he would *parley*[9]. The guards *lowered*[10] their arms and disposed themselves to listen to him. All of a sudden he *bared*[11] his sword, and united with his four champions *fell upon them*[12], without other intention than that of *terrifying them*[13], to give time to a detachment of the garrison to sally and to second him. Thus it was done: the generous father *was* [*came*] snatched *from* [*to*] the hands of his *detainers* [*satellites*], and conducted *within* [*between*] the walls in triumph, as he well deserved.

¹mossa guerra al. ²gravissime. ³picchetto. ⁴trucidare.
⁵posto che. ⁶piazza. ⁷trattare. ⁸ti provocassi. ⁹parlamentare.
¹⁰calarono. ¹¹snudò. ¹²piombò loro addosso. ¹³sbigottirle.

¹Parse this. ⁵Of what verb is posto the pass. part.? — The
expression corresponds to our "putting the case." ⁶The Fr. *place*,
and our *place*, in the sense of *fortified place*. ⁷More literally
"treating of." What would have rendered this less easy of translation? ⁸What is the connexion between *provoke* and *incite*? Where
has *provoke* this primary sense in English? In our Authorised
Version of the Bible, where however we find it used in both senses:
Heb. x, 24, and Gal. v, 26. ¹¹From nudo. ¹²Piombare (from
piombo = lead) = to come down like lead. — Parse this phrase.

---

24. The Passions sacrificed to the public Weal.

Being-dead the celebrated Bertrand du Guesclin,
Charles V, called the Wise, offered the sword of constable to Enguerrand de Couci, who refused it. "This
charge," said he generously to his prince, "requires
a soul full of *vigour*¹, and my age, sire, permits me
not to have aught except zeal; it would be shame for
me to succeed to a Bertrand without having his talents."
The Monarch refused not to *satisfy*² him, and restricted himself *merely*³ to asking that he *would suggest*⁴
to him person reputed by him the most worthy to *fill*
[*cover*] that post. "Sire," rejoined Enguerrand, "elect
Oliver de Clisson." Charles remained astonished at
such words, well knowing that this Oliver was *precisely*⁵ the greatest enemy that the De Couci had.
"I confess to you the truth," he said to him, "that
I should rather have thought that you would have
suggested to me a certain your kinsman, of whom you

cannot ignore the ability." — "I know of whom *you mean*[6] to speak to me," resumed Enguerrand; "*I agree*[7] that he is an *able*[8] man and *known*[9] for some luminous actions; but let us not *delude* [*illude*][10] ourselves, sire, he comes after Clisson." — This is truly a sacrificing *one's own*[11] passions to the good of the state.

[1] robustezza. [2] appagare. [3] soltanto. [4] volesse suggerire. [5] appunto. [6] volete. [7] accordo. [8] valente. [9] noto. [11] le proprie.

[2] The root is pago = satisfied; hence also pagare = to pay, i. e. to satisfy in respect of a money claim. [4] Chiedere governs this in the subj. — Volesse is a courteous form of speech, as in French *qu'il voulut bien*. [6] Voler parlare di, voler dire = to mean; as in French. [8] From valere = to be worth: but the sense is not that of our *worthy;* — power, rather than moral goodness, is the idea in Italian. [10] Illudersi implies self-deception; deludere deception of another. As in French.

---

25. The Heroine of Leucate.

Barri de Saint-Aunez, governor for Henry IV at Leucate, having heard, in 1550, the disembarkation made by a body of Spanish troops in aid of the enemy, departed from the city with the design to communicate a project of his to the Duke of Montmorenci, commander general of the province. The factious *on the road*[1] made him prisoner, and united to the disembarked Spaniards, attempted immediately a *sudden attack*[2] against Leucate, persuaded that having in their power the governor, the fortress would not have delayed to surrender itself.

Scarcely arrived, they put into activity every expedient *whereby*[3] to succeed in the intent; but Constance de Cezeli, wife of the governor, had taken the post of her husband. She assembled garrison and inhabitants; *reminded all with masculine energy of their duty*[4], placed herself at their head with the pike in the hand, and infused even into the pusillanimous the most intrepid daring. The enemies *consequently had to adopt the measure*[5] of commencing *a formal siege* [*the siege in the forms*]. The time was passing, and their efforts were turning out vain: wherever they might present themselves, they *were* [*came*] ignominiously *repulsed*[6]. Stung by the shame of seeing themselves *overcome*[7] by a woman, they resolved to *send her an envoy*[8] with the declaration that if she *continued* [*should have continued*] to defend herself, they *would cause to be hanged* [*would have made hang*[9]] her husband opposite to the walls of the city. "The considerable goods which I hold," she answered, "I have already offered them and I offer them again for his *ransom*[10]; but *let it never be*[11] that I should purchase by a vile act a life which he *would reproach*[12] to me, and which *he would blush*[13] to preserve at such price: never shall it be that I dishonour it by betraying my country and my king."

In place of *changing counsel*[14] at a so heroic answer, those barbarians, having-executed first one last attempt against the fortress, which turned out to them not better than the others, *caused to be ignominiously hanged* [*made vilely hang*] the unhappy governor, and raised afterwards the siege. The garrison of the city wanted immediately to do the same towards the lord de Loupian, fallen into its hands; but the magnanimous *governess*[15] generously prevented their revenge.

This great woman bore not that title except for being wife of the governor; Henry IV however, *since*[16] he *learned* [*knew*] how *she had behaved herself*[17], sent her the patent, and assured the same grade to her son, after *her*[18] death.

The latter, *having-succeeded*[19] to his mother, imitated her intrepidity and fidelity; and when the general Serbelloni, in 1637, caused to be invested Leucate and *feared*[20] the slowness of a siege, having attempted to corrupt the commandant by promising him *brilliant*[21] advantages if he would have chosen to embrace the *cause*[22] of the Spaniards, *this one*[23] sent him for *sole*[24] and decisive answer the succinct story of the mode by which his *parents*[25] had defended the fortress.

[1]per istrada. [2]colpo di mano. [3]onde. [4]ricordo a tutti con virile energia il loro dovere. [5]pertanto dovettero appigliarsi al partito. [6]respinti. [7]superati. [8]spedirle un parlamentario. [9]impiccare. [10]riscatto. [11]non fia mai. [12]rinfaccerebbe. [13]avrebbe rossore. [14]mutare d'avviso. [15]governatrice. [16]da che. [17]erasi diportata. [18]la di lei. [19]subentrato. [20]paventò. [21]luminosi. [22]partito. [23]questi. [24]unica. [25]genitori.

[2]The Fr. *coup de main;* no exact equivalent in English. [4], [5]Parse these, and notice the cases connected with ricordare. — Virile and maschio (not mascolino) are the proper terms in speaking of character. — Appigliarsi = to catch at, cling to; from pigliare = to take. [8]What is the term for *parley?* [9]Impiccare = to put to death by hanging. Appendere = to hang in a general sense. [11]Fia is used in the historical and poetical style for sarà; but the imperative is often the best English equivalent. [12]Like our "he would throw it in my teeth." [13]Rossore is of course from —? [15]Governess = instructress = aja or istitutrice. [18]Why not sua? [21]Luminosi is from —? [22]Notice the various meanings of this word. [24]Could you say unique here in English? Why not? In what does the use of the word differ in the two

languages? [25] Parents (Eng.) = father and mother: (Fr.) = father and mother, and relations; parenti (Ital.) = relations.

---

26. THE FRENCHWOMAN OF SPARTAN HEART.

The mother of a renowned family had five sons in the army of Henry IV of France, who emulated the distinguished valour of their father, militant he also under the same banners. She had reserved of them a sixth at her side, as the youngest and of a very delicate *constitution* [1]. At the battle of Arcis the marquis her husband and the five sons all perished gloriously, almost under the eyes of their sovereign. The announcement of this terrible *news dealt* [2] a mortal blow to the sensibility of the lady; but *there quickly revived* [*delayed not to reanimate itself*] that love of country which in her vanquished every other passion. *She has brought to her an armour* [3] which she had *just* [4] caused to be *made for* [*adapted to*] the last of her sons, and with the heart of true Spartan girds him therewith with her own hand and breaks out into such words: "Go, my son, avenge thy father and thy brothers, or die with them for thy native-land." Then, with dry eyes, she herself hastens the departure of this only son, of this *last* [*extreme*] hope of a *tottering lineage* [5]; and because, mounted on horseback, he goes repeating to her saddest farewell: "Think rather of glory," says to him this heroine, "and render thyself worthy either of my weeping, if thou diest, or of my jubilation, if thou returnest."

Last *offshoot* [6] of so many illustrious warriors, and son of a woman who had in bosom the heart of the

Scipios, he knew in such wise to signalize himself in the army of Henry IV, that he attracted to himself the *eyes* [*looks*] of this great prince. Surprised by his valour, he asked who he might be; and having-heard his name: "Truly!" he exclaimed, "this house is a *nursery*[7] of heroes; it is needful that to me be preserved jealously this precious offshoot." The young warrior, not less brave, but more fortunate however than his brothers and than his father, ended that was the campaign, returned to his castle, and in the throwing himself on the neck of the *illustrious*[8] mother: "*Receive*[9]," he said to her, "*into* [*between*] your arms a son who loves you." — "I embrace with jubilation a son who honours me," returned the marchioness. Owes to him its origin one of the most illustrious families of the *district*[10] of Avignon.

[1] complessione. [2] nuova portò. [3] si fa presentare un' armatura. [4] di fresco. [5] vacillante prosapia. [6] rampollo. [7] semenzaio. [8] inclita. [9] accogliete. [10] contado.

[This anecdote is entirely in the noble style; many of the words would be affected in ordinary prose.] [2] Nuova, used of *one* piece of intelligence, is in the sing. as in French. [3] Armatura = a suit of armour. [7] From semenza = seed; like our *seed-plot*. [9] This word includes the idea of welcome. So "gli fece mille accoglienze = he received him with a thousand demonstrations of welcome."

27. The Victim of his Country.

The eve of the fight of Clostercamp, the captain d'Assas of the regiment of Auvergne, in the silence of a night *illumined*[1] by the lunar *glimmer*, *advanced*[2], in order better to discover the *ground*[3] and the *hostile*[4] positions.· At short distance from his body he perceived that the enemies, *hidden*[5] in the woods, already meditated to surprise the French army. Scarcely had he made this discovery, he *was [came] suddenly caught*[6] by a picquet of advanced guards who threatened to kill him on the fact, *if [when]* he should have given the least sign by which they should have been discovered. Already ten bayonets *were pointed*[7] at his breast; but *what can*[8] the fear of death in a heart sacred to the native-land? Without *a moment's trepidation*[9], the captain cried: "*Up*[10], Auvergne! the enemy is here:" to terminate these words and to die was all one for him. But meanwhile the regiment perceived that the enemy was present; the drum was beaten, all the body placed itself in *battle array*[11], sustained the first shock, the assault *was [came]* repulsed and the assailants *pursued*[12]; this luminous advantage however by the regiment could not be celebrated in other manner, except with the tears shed over the *corpse*[13] of its generous captain.

[1] illustrata. [2] barlume, innoltrossi. [3] terreno. [4] nemiche. [5] appiattati. [6] improvvisamente còlto. [7] stavano appuntate. [9] trepidare un momento. [10] all' erta. [11] battaglia. [12] inseguiti. [13] cadavere.

[1] From lustro. [2] Oltre = forward, beyond, is the root of innoltrarsi. [3] A more restricted word than terra. [5] From piatto = flat; appiattarsi = to squat. [6] The circumflex accent, though not necessary, is useful to distinguish the pass. part. of cogliere from colto, adj. = cultivated. [8] Che può — ? is equivalent to che potere ha — ? [9] Parse this. It cannot be literally rendered for want of the verb to trepidate. [10] Our adj. alert is from the same root.

28. THE PIEDMONTESE HERO.

A sergeant of the Piedmontese guards, at the head
of some soldiers, watched at the custody of a *mine*,
placed under[1] an advanced work of the citadel, when
the French *were besieging*[2] Turin, the year 1640.
He knew that sundry hostile companies had possessed
themselves of the upper part, and had established
there a *redoubt*[3]. He doubted not that the overturn
of this work *would*[4] retard the surrender of the
fortress. The *mine*[5] was *in readiness*[6], and he had
with him the *match*[7]. What does the generous soldier?
he commands the subalterns to withdraw themselves,
charges them to beg the King, in his stead, that *he
will*[8] protect the wife and the children; and when he
knows to be alone *in* [*at*] the peril, *sets*[9] fire to the
mine, and *is blown up* [*leaps into air*] with his enemies,
victim of the native-land.

[1] sotterraneo, sottoposto ad.   [2] stringeano d'assedio.   [3] ridotto
[4] non fosse per.   [5] mina.   [6] in pronto.   [7] razzo.   [8] voglia.   [9] appicca.

[4] This non is merely an idiomatic expletive after dubitò. —
Literally, "was about to retard."   [6] Readiness = promptness, is
prontezza.   [8] Voglia is here equivalent to *will be pleased to*.

29. THE GENEROUS GRENADIER.

Finding itself Lille *surrounded by siege*[1], in the
year 1708, it imported very much to the commander
to *know*[2] the progresses of an *entrenchment*[3] raised
by the enemy; but this discovery was of the most
perilous. To whomever *indiscriminately*[4] should have

succeeded in it, he promised a hundred louis. Five soldiers *dared* [*faced*]⁵, the one after the other, the enterprise, nor more were they seen to return. *Offered himself*⁶ a sixth, and this was a grenadier of great hopes; the garrison saw him not depart without much *regret*⁷. Awaited with impatience, and *interposed*⁸ a long delay to the return, he was held for dead and deservedly *bewailed*⁹ by all. He however reappeared, and rendered minute account of the object for which he had been despatched. On the *strength* [*support*]¹⁰ of his narrations, the general executed a sally and *carried*¹¹ an extreme harm to the enemy. Returned into the fortress in triumph, he assembled the garrison, made come to him the brave man to whom principally was owing the *issue*¹² of this undertaking, and presented to him the promised recompense: "A thousand thanks, my general," said he: *"one goes not there*¹³ for money." The grade of *officer was the single prize*¹⁴ that he bent himself to accept.

¹stretta d'assedio. ²conoscere. ³trincea. ⁴indistintamente. ⁵affrontarono. ⁶si esibì. ⁷rincrescimento. ⁸frapposto. ⁹compianto. ¹⁰appoggio. ¹¹recò. ¹²esito ¹³non si va colà. ¹⁴unico premio.

⁶Esibire is to *offer*, not to *exhibit;* this last is esporre. ⁸Frapposto = posto fra = placed between. ⁹What is the more usual meaning of compiangere? To pity = compassionate = suffer or weep with. ¹¹Recare = to bring; recarsi = to repair (Fr. *se rendre*).

30. The Imperturbables.

The year 1756, in the fight of Minorca, a ball carried away the right arm *of* [*to*] an *artilleryman*[1], in the
act that he was about to *set* [*give*] fire to the cannon.
The wounded man, as if nothing had happened to him,
picked up [*raised*] from the ground the *match*[2] with
the left hand, and continuing his operation, said
somewhat angry[3]: "*Perhaps these fellows think*[4] that
I have but one arm?"
Not dissimilar to him, the year 1781, a grenadier
of the regiment Soissons, *seeing one of his legs shattered* [*seeing himself shattered*[5] *a leg*] by a blow of
cannon, seated himself tranquil[3], finished to cut the
flesh by which still it hung, threw it into sea, and *re-
loading as usual*[6] his gun, said with effusion of heart:
"Praise to God, there remain to me still two arms
and one leg to serve my country and my King."

[1] artigliere. [2] miccia. [4] credono forse costoro. [5] fracassata.
[6] ricaricando al solito.

[3] Two instances of a frequent idiom, by which the noun is
qualified by an adjective, rather than the verb, as in English, by an
adverb. [4] Costoro, &c. are contemptuous in familiar, tho' not in
noble language. — Forse, in interrogative sentences, is an expletive.

31. Mecænas.

One of the greatest *signs*[1] of love to the Sovereign
is the courage to tell him the truth. Often disorders
take root[2] in a State because *they are unknown by
him who*[3] has in hand the *reins*[4] of it. Besides, the

greater number of such persons loves not to hear things which *may disturb*[5] that species of beatitude which *is* [*comes*] promised them by the eminence of the grade, and rare *too*[6] are the zealots who may expose themselves, by *disturbing it*[7], to the peril either to fall into disgrace, or to multiply to themselves the enemies who are inseparable from reforms.

When Augustus was about to mount on the throne, Mecænas had the frankness to give him this lesson: "A virtuous conduct will be for you a guard more secure than that of all your legions. The best rule, in *matter*[8] of government, is to acquire oneself the friendship of the people. It is needful that the prince do to his subjects that which he would wish done to himself if he were subject. Avoid the title of Monarch or of King; content yourself with the name of Cæsar, adding to it that of Emperor, or any other, proper to conciliate to yourself respect, without provoking *against* [*to*] you *odium*[9]."

Mecænas preserved always the same style towards the emperor. He knew so to couple sincerity with sweetness and with prudence, that he had attained even to reprove *him for* [*to him*] his *faults*[10], *without his taking offence at it*[11]. He passes one day through the public place and sees Cæsar seated at his tribunal who judges some delinquents in ferocious air. He takes quickly a tablet; writes on it: "Withdraw thyself, O executioner"; and throws it at his feet. Augustus picks it up, reads it, rises at once, descends and departs. What pleasure to be Mecænases, and Mecænases friends of such Cæsars!

---

[1] contrassegni. [2] allignano. [3] s'ignorano da chi. [4] redini. [5] tur-

bino. ⁶poi. ⁷alterarla. ⁸proposito. ⁹odiosita. ¹⁰falli. ¹¹senza ch'egli se ne offendesse.

⁷This verb, properly *to alter*, is also used in the sense given above. — Alterarsi, v. refl., is *to become angry*. ¹¹Parse this, and note where it differs from the English.

32. THE SINCERE COURTIERS.

Charles VII, King of France, who without the happy *circumstance* [*combination*] of having great men at his side would have abandoned armies and kingdom in prey to themselves to immerse himself in pleasures, one day that he was *engrossed*¹ in the enjoying a feast given by himself, answered to the general La Hire, who had interrogated him on points of the highest importance: "What think you of this *amusement* [*diversion*]?" — "I think", rejoined promptly the general, "that one cannot lose the kingdom more merrily."

Was² not less free the speech of Lansac to the King Charles IX, whose sanguinary spirit manifested itself but too much even against beasts. One of the chief pleasures of this cruel soul was *to cut off*³ at one single blow the head to the asses or pigs which by chance he had met *on road*⁴. Lansac, his favourite, to whom nevertheless *were vividly displeasing*⁵ such brutalities, surprised him one day in the act that *he rushed*⁶ with the sword in the hand against *the animal he rode*⁷. *He restrained him*⁸ and asked him gravely: "Sire, *what variance is ever arisen*⁹ between Your Most Christian Majesty and my mule?"

¹occupatissimo. ³l'abbattere. ⁴per via. ⁵vivamente dispiaceano.

⁶si avventava. ⁷la sua cavalcatura. ⁸lo rattenne. ⁹qual disparere
e mai insorto.

² Why this inversion? First because it brings the idea of truthful freedom into the most prominent place; next because it facili-
tates the grammatical construction by placing the antecedent next
to the relative. Always try to account to yourself for inversions,
and when you see reason use them freely in your own compositions;
much of the idiomatic grace of the language depends on them.
³ Why not d'abbattere? Neither form is incorrect: but Italians instinctively prefer to treat infinitives as nouns, when a previous
noun is said to consist in the action denoted by the infinitive. In
this sentence, a *pleasure* is described as consisting in *cutting off*;
pleasure being a noun, *to cut off* is elegantly made so too. The
use of the gerund answers the same purpose in English. ⁷Cavalcare
(from cavallo) = to ride; cavalcatura = the animal ridden. ⁹Parere
= to seem, is also used as a noun meaning *opinion; i. e. what
seems* right or true. Disparere is therefore *dissimilarity of opinion.*

33. Song-chi Chinese Heroine.

The Emperor Khan-gai-ti was walking·in *a court*¹
of the *seraglio*², accompanied by *some*³ of his wives.
The gate of the park, in which *were shut up*⁴ the
wild beasts, being open by accident, a bear issued
thence which came *hurriedly*⁵ towards the Sovereign.
The women, at the first seeing him, fled terrified; one
of them however, by name Song-chi, in place of thinking to save herself, had the courage to place herself
impetuously between the Emperor and the wild beast.
The bear, which was not *very hungry*⁶, given some
steps around the court, returned *spontaneously*⁷ between
his *bars*⁸. Meanwhile the monarch, surprised at the intrepidity of this woman, asked her why, instead of

fleeing like the others, she should have chosen a post so perilous. "I am not except a simple woman," she answered; "my life matters very little to the felicity of the state; yours, on the contrary, is precious, nor ought I to hesitate to sacrifice it to you." — *Let not any one be amazed*⁹ at such generous answer. Who knows the history of that nation, knows that a Chinese lady thinks and talks often better than *some of our European ladies* [*some one*¹⁰ *our European*].

¹ un cortile. ² serraglio. ³ taluna. ⁴ stavano rinchiuse. ⁵ frettoloso. ⁶ affamato. ⁷ spontaneo. ⁸ cancelli. ⁹ non si stupisca. ¹⁰ qualche.

¹ La corte = the court. Il cortile = the court-yard. — "La corte della regina è radunata nel cortile del palazzo." ² The double r points to serrare as the root. ³ A singular form in a plural sense. ⁴, ⁵, ⁷ Recall the former notes on stare, and on the substitution of adjectives for adverbs. I hope you continually refer, by the help of the index, to previous notes; repetitions and references would swell this book to a most inconvenient size. ⁶ Nearly corresponding to *famished*, but not necessarily quite so strong. ⁹ Parse this, and account for si.

34. PHILIP THE MACEDONIAN.

There cannot *be called to mind*¹ the Princes who were friends of their subjects, without that there should present himself to the spirit Philip, father of Alexander the Macedonian. The love to the truth and the *mastery* [*lordship*] of himself rendered him worthy to be king. After the victory of Chæronea, he visited the field of battle, and set himself to insult brutally corpses

and prisoners. Demaratus, one of this number, could
not *restrain himself*[2] from saying to him: "Why *will*[3]
you be a Thersites" (Greek warrior, killed by Achilles
for his stinging tongue), "when instead you might be
an Agamemnon?" Philip, having-heard this reproof,
made at once *be replaced* [*replace*] in liberty Demaratus, and treated with *gentleness*[4] his unfortunate companions.

Not otherwise he comported himself that day in
which he was occupied in observing the sale which
was being made[5] of some slaves. *He was reclining*[6],
perhaps without thinking of it, in an indecent posture,
of the which thing one of them advertised him: "Let
liberty be *quickly*[7] given him", said the King; "I
knew not that he was of the number of my friends."

It happened also one time that a poor woman *incited*[8] him to take into consideration an affair *critical
to her* [*for her decisive*], and to *deign*[9] to do her
justice. It seemed that to the King was wanting the
courage to *face the trouble*[10] by which he was menaced
consenting [*adhering*] to her *urgencies*[11], and under
pretext of not having the necessary time, *he put off
this miserable woman*[12] from one day to the other.
She, weary at last, had the courage to tell him: "If
you will not hear me, cease then to be King." Philip
comprehended all the force of this expression, and
gave her at once *hearing*[13] with the most exact
patience.

There came another woman to implore justice, at
the *tiresome*[14] moment- in which he was risen from a
sumptuous[15] banquet. He listens to her with distraction
and *decides against her* [*gives her wrong*] *precipitately*[16].
— "I *appeal*[17]", said she in anger, "*from* this unjust

sentence." — "And to whom *do you assert the right* [*pretend you*] to appeal?" — "I appeal", *returned she*[18], "to Philip fasting." These words recall him to his duty; he examines with *consideration*[19] the affair, and revokes the given sentence.

[1]rammemorarsi. [2]trattenersi. [3]volete. [4]dolcezza. [5]si stava facendo. [6]giacea. [7]tosto. [8]stimolasse. [9]piegarsi. [10]affrontare la noia. [11]premure. [12]rimettea questa misera. [13]ascolto. [14]importuno. [15]lauto. [16]a precipizio. [17]mi appello di. [18]soggiunse [19]ponderazione.

[1]Give the root. [4]The literal meaning? [6]More usually *was lying*. [8]Avvenne che governs this in the subj.; but the indic. would not be wrong. [10]Affrontare is from fronte; to come *a fronte* (face to face) with anything. Noia is the Fr. *ennui*, the Engl. *annoyance*, but does not precisely correspond to either; translate it according to the sense. [11]From the verb premere = to press; as a reflected verb with the dative case frequently used to denote *pressing* concern. "Gli preme molto che ciò accada = that this should happen is a matter of importance and anxiety to him." Premura is sometimes *eagerness;* but the same idea always underlies it. [15]More idiomatic than sontuoso in speaking of a banquet. [16]Literally *headlong*. [19]From what root? Pondo; ponderare (Eng. *ponder*), ponderazione.

35. Ardisheer Babegan, Sophi[1] of Persia.

Ardisheer Babegan, the first king of the dynasty of the Sassanids in Persia, who mounted on the throne the year of our era 226, was a king so *devoted* [*applied*] to his own duty, that there was not who in exactness surpassed him. It will suffice to say that the last of his actions, every day, was *to write*[2] minutely *what*[3] in that he had done, be it as prince, be it as private person, reproving to himself his own faults, although covered by his eminent virtues; and this journal *came down* [4] even to our days, *as also* [*not less than*] another book of his with the title: *Rules to live well*, compiled in order to serve *as guide* [5] to the princes *at once* [6] and to the peoples. He repeated often that "the subject is submissive when the King is just," — that "the most wicked of all the princes is *he who is* [*the*] feared by the good and [*the*] *acceptable* [7] to the perverse;" to the judges *too* [8] who represented him, he used to say frequently: "Employ not the sword, when the cane suffices."

[1] soft. [2] lo scrivere. [3] quanto. [4] pervenne. [5] di norma. [6] insieme. [7] gradito. [8] poi.

[2] Why do you treat this infin. as a noun? [3] Literally "as much as;" one of the most idiomatic Ital. pronouns. [4] Pervenire = to come down: tramandare (you had it in a former lesson) = to hand down. [5] Norma, literally a rule or square. Hence our *normal*. [6] Literally —? [8] As an adverb of sequence poi (Fr. *puis*) means *then*, *next*, *afterwards*; as an expletive it must be translated according to the sense, and often (as here) has no precise equivalent.

36. Titus Flavius Vespasian.

Titus Flavius Vespasian, born the ninth year of our era, *was sixty years old* [*had of them sixty*] when he was raised to the empire. He opened the glorious career with a difficult and delicate project, that of bridling the *arrogance* [*petulance*] and the excesses of the military who *domineered over* [*importuned*] the *peaceful* [*placid*] citizens and desolated the poor *peasantry* [1].

He succeeded in it combining energy with prudence.
It was not little for him to be able to remedy the *ef-
feminacy*[2] of the officers, first *rock*[3] of the military
discipline. To one of these gentlemen, who had presented himself to thank him *for* [*of*] an advancement
of grade, all fragrant of odorous perfumes, he said
frowning: "I would that thou *smelledst*[4] of garlic,
rather than *savour*[4] of a thousand odours." He extended *then*[0] the reform to all the orders of the State:
shortened *legal processes* [*the forensic*[5] *method*], prevented
chicanery[6] and *artifice*[7]; and *since*[8], also in those
days, a *swarm*[9] of greedy usurers *buzzed*[10] around
the dissolute youth, and by loans at exorbitant profits
desolated the best families, he prescribed that whoever
might have lent to the sons at illegal interest, could
no more *reclaim*[11] either profits or capital.

Thus *it happened*[12] that the sweetness of his character, that clemency for which he became famous,
never *violated* [*offended*] justice. There was not in the
world person who surpassed him in the exercise of a
certain bounty which one might call imperial. Far
from preventing with death the plots against himself,
he was lavish in signal benefits towards whoever *had
incurred his suspicion of being a plotter*[13]; by which
moderation he disarmed all. Being one day warned
by his dearest friends that *he should be on his guard*[14]
against Metius Pomposianus, because there *had arisen
a report* [*was diffused the voice*] that his horoscope had
promised him the empire, he raised him at once to the
honour of the consulate, pronouncing those divine words:
"If Metius shall become in my stead emperor, he will
remember at least that I have done to him some good.
I pity those who would occupy my post, they are

madmen {who aspire to· bear a very heavy burden."
And when his *intimates rallied him*[15], and when *under-
hand*[16] there were affixed to the corners of Rome
satires against him, that great soul *amused himself*[17]
to imagine some *squib which should serve him as excuse
with the indiscreet jesters*[18], and gave to this squib
the same publicity.

How much was he alien from ambition! The King
of the Parthians having sent to him a letter with this
address: "Arsaces king of kings to Flavius Vespasian,"
it *pleased* [*was grateful to*] the Emperor to answer him
simply: "Flavius Vespasian to Arsaces king of kings."
His predecessors had shown themselves very *osten-
tatious*[19] of titles; he refused *long*[20] that even of *father
of his country* which he had so well merited. His
pride[21] was all placed in the protecting arts and
sciences; he held that they could not make progresses
if one was not liberal with those who professed them,
and it was *therefore*[22] that to a single man of letters
he *assigned as much as* [*arrived to assign even to*] a
hundred thousand annual *sesterces*[23]. *Nevertheless*[24] he
was not towards them *prepossessed so as to*[25] caress
them when they might merit reprehension; rather he
banished from Rome several of them as disseminators
of *bad*[26] examples and of dangerous principles. Whoever
had made some useful discovery, some advantageous
invention, or composed any choice work, was sure of
a pension, or of other *abundant*[27] gift. The very me-
chanical arts found in him a protector, *altogether*[28] as
if they were liberal arts; and to a certain mechanic
who had suggested a project *by which*[29] to transport,
with light expence, into the Capitol two columns of
enormous weight, he accorded the same *recompense*[30]

as if the project had already been executed, saying: "*Worthy people*[31] must live." He embellished *then*[0] Rome and the cities of the State; some of them he erected, others of them fortified, improving everywhere the public roads. The empire under him was *flourishing* [*florid*] internally, was respected and feared *without*[32]. After ten years of reign, struck by grave intestinal malady, he continued to apply himself to the public affairs, as if he were *well, as if he would not even*[33] grant himself the time to die; and if his affectionate friends conjured him to think at last of himself, he repeated the *so*[34] celebrated saying: "An Emperor *must*[35] die standing." The Romans used *to set*[36] amongst the *gods*[37] these their *rulers*[38]. Alluding to such for him langhable fashion, he died perfectly tranquil as he had lived, with the jest on the lip: "*I also am shortly to*[39] become a god."

---

[1] rustici. [2] mollezza. [3] scoglio. [4] puzzare — sapere. [0] quindi. [5] forense. [6] cavillazione. [7] raggirọ. [8] poiche. [9] sciame. [10] ronzava. [11] ripetere. [12] ne nacque. [13] gli fosse caduto in sospetto d'insidiatore. [14] stesse in guardia. [15] famigliari lo motteggiavano. [16] di soppiatto. [17] si dilettava. [18] scherzo che gli valesse a discolpa presso gl'indiscreti dileggiatori. [19] fastosi. [20] a lungo. [21] fasto. [22] perciò. [23] sesterzi. [24] tuttavia. [25] prevenuto talmente di. [26] tristi. [27] larghissimo. [28] affatto. [29] onde. [30] retribuzione. [31] la brava gente. [32] al di fuori. [33] sano, quasi non volesse neppure. [34] tanto. [35] deve. [36] riporre. [37] numi. [38] regnanti. [39] sto in breve anch' io per.

---

[3] This word, though not confined to that sense, is always preferred when a *rock* is spoken of as an *obstacle* or *cause of wreck.* [4] Puzzare is always used of a *bad* smell. — Note this use of sapere = to *savour* physically or morally. "Questo budino sa di cennamella, this pudding savours of cinnamon." — "Costui mi sa di pedante, this man savours of pedantry." [7] Literally *twisting* and *turning.* [11] Also very commonly *to repeat.* [13], [18], [33], [39] Parse.

6 *

[17] This verb often refers to amusement. So also un libro dilette-
vole = an amusing book. [19], [21] Fasto is more properly *ostentation;*
but the sense sometimes requires *pride.* [24] Tuttavia = nevertheless
= for all that. [25] Prevenire (Fr. *prévenir*) = to anticipate, to
prepossess. The Eng. *prevent* is from the same root; trace the
connexion of meaning. [26] Often *wicked* as well as *sad ;* quel tristo
= *that wretch.* [27] Remember our *largess.* [28] More frequently used
in negative sentences; "non mi piace affatto = I do not like it
at all." [29] Note the continual and varied use of this relative con-
junction. [30] Ricompensa is more usual; but retribuzione admits,
as here, of a favourable sense. [34] More idiomatic and expressive
than sì. [38] A word confined to the noble style; really the pres.
part. of regnare.

37. Titus Vespasian.

Titus Vespasian, son of the preceding, occupied the
throne of his father and emulated his virtues. More
popular [1] still than he, he confirmed the benefits and
the privileges granted to the people by his predecessors,
studied to keep it *amused [distracted]* by frequent spectacles, of the which he left to its *will* [2] the choice, and
permitted that every *man of the people* [1], raised to any
charge, should profit by his own baths, even at that
time in which he himself was using them.

With severest laws he prevented the corruptions of
the judges and the venality of the *informers* [3], condemn-
ing those who accused *by profession* [4] to be whipped
through the city, sold *after the [to]* manner of slaves
and *banished to* [5] uninhabited islands. *It is not therefore to be wondered at* [6] if he were very *wary* [7] before
lending faith to the accusations, and to those even
which regarded his own person; nor was he ever seen
to be disturbed [8], whatever might be the motive that

he might have to complain of any one: "I do not aught," he said, "that is worthy of reprehension; why then, when some one calumniates me, am I to be angry?" Two patricians were *convicted*[9] of having conspired against his life. The same evening in which the conspiracy *was* [*came*] discovered, he invited them to supper; the day after, a public spectacle *coming round*[10], he *would have*[11] them seated at his side, and being himself thus in midst, talked with them with the greatest affability.

What celestial propensity in that soul to do the good! If some day was so sinister for him that there presented itself not to him the opportunity to *do good*[12], he *addressed* [*turned*] to the bystanders those memorable words: "My friends, I have lost a day." In the public calamities he was generous prince, was tender father, and to re-establish the public edifices *burnt down*[13], he exposed to the sale the furniture of his own palace. This man precious to the empire, seized by illness, in the fresh age of forty years, ceased to live, raising to the heaven the languishing eyes, and complaining *of*[14] this alone that he could not more *do good*[12] to *mankind* [*humanity*].

---

[1]popolare. [2]arbitrio. [3]delatori. [4]per mestiere. [5]rilegati in [6]non è quindi a stupire. [7]guardingo. [8]turbarsi. [9]convinti [10]ricorrendo. [11]volle. [12]giovare. [13]incendiati. [14]per.

---

[1]Popolare, adj. = I. favourable to the people, as here = II. in favour with the people. = III. (used as a noun) man of the people. [2]Arbitrio, will exercised in choice. Give the Eng. words from this root. [5]Rilegare, to banish to some place where the exile must remain, but within which he was free. — This word, from its resemblance to the Fr. *relier*, is ridiculously confused with *legare*, and English pupils talk of sending a book to be rilegato. [6]Parse.

[7] From the root of what verb? [8] Note here and elsewhere the substitution of the reflected for the passive form; it is frequent in
emotional verbs. [9] Convincere is usually to convict; **persuadere to
convince.** [10] Our *to recur* is literally *to come back in course.* [11]]
hope you never omit accounting for every recurrence of volere,
dovere, potere.

38. TRAJAN.

Marcus Ulpius Crinitus Trajan mounted *on [to]* the
throne of Rome the year 93 of the vulgar era. *There
never was in the*[1] world a man who united so much
power to so much *familiarity*[2] and affability with his
dependants. Nor this through effect of *ostentation*[3], as
in *many [several]*, but of character and of principles;
since that his cordial *familiarity*[2] lasted as long as life,
nor belied itself *on [in]* any occasion.

The first *sign*[4] which he gave to the Romans of
the high contempt in which he held exterior greatnesses
isolated from merit, was his *entrance on foot*[5] into the
capital, when he entered it in quality of monarch. If
he went out of house, he tolerated not that any should
accompany him to save him from the *press*[6] of the
people which *crowded around him*[7]; and it was indeed[8] a surprising thing to see the master of the then
known world *stand in the street*[9] confused with the
others, amongst the carriages, waiting calm that they
should accord him the passage. Of jovial humour, of
witty and *courteous*[10] conversation, it was a delight to
find oneself, especially at table, with him. His ordinary
recreations [pastimes] consisted in the changing object
of occupation; but if *however*[8] sometimes he wanted
to repose the spirit, he set himself, for example, to

row a boat, taking his friends *pleasuring*[11], because
he was emperor and had some. *Pleasant was it to see
him repair*[12] to pay them visit, as if he were a private person; conduct of them three or four together in
his own *coach, or else*[13] be the third or the fourth of
the *party*[14] in the coach of another; *betake himself*[15]
to supper invited into their house, and when they held
a family council for domestic affairs, assist thereat he
also and allege his opinion, *just as if an immediate interest of his own were being treated of* [*as if one
treated precisely of one his immediate interest*].

Presented himself to him a senator? His predecessors would have well guarded themselves from moving;
but Trajan rose from his *seat, went to meet him*[16], embraced him, and when some *petty insolent man*[17]
whispered him in the ear that *that so much*[18] courtesy
in a sovereign degenerated into a species of *degra-
dation*[19]: "I will", he answered, "do to all that which
I would that an emperor should do to me, *if* [*when*]
fate had made me subject" *So far* [*To so much*]
pushed he the contempt for distinctions and for pomp,
that there was not thing which provoked him more to
laughter as much as to hear the honours which were
rendered "to the bits of bronze or of marble"; such
were his expressions respecting those statues which *by
main force*[20] the Romans wanted to raise to him.

The *one*[21] scope which he prefixed to himself, go-
verning the empire, was that of making himself beloved,
and he *attained*[22] it to perfection. In a *worthless*[23]
monarch, that so much familiarity would have certainly
turned out dangerous; in Trajan, *full*[24] of merits,
whose great *achievements* [*enterprises*] had covered him
with glory, it awoke instead wonder, affection, venera-

tion. Father and brother of his subjects, such was the
trust by him reposed in their heart, that he *attained* [25]
even to abolish *every [whatever]* [26] penalty menaced by
the laws against the crimes of *high treason* [27]; an abo-
lition, of which the sole thought would suffice to appal
every prince, but which serves *it alone* [28] to form the
eulogium of Marcus Trajan.

How could one ever conspire against him? Sura
was the first of his confidants. Be it truth, be it envy
which moved the courtiers to speak, they accuse him to
the Emperor as if he *wove plots* [29] against his life.
Trajan had on that very day received an invitation to
betake himself to supper with him. The Emperor repairs thither not accompanied by guards; begs the
host, before placing himself at table, that he send for
his surgeon and for his barber, and when he has them,
causes *to be trimmed* [30] by the one his eyebrows and
to be shaved [31] by the other his beard. Afterwards he
descends into the domestic bath, and then sits *cheer-
ful* [32] at the table, surrounded by the *guests* [33]. A confidence pushed to such a point made fall the weapons
from the hand, whatever had been the perverse intention of him who had *grasped* [34] them.

Difficult undertaking it would be to describe the
cities, the edifices, the monuments, the roads, the bridges,
the dams [35], the aqueducts which through all the
extent of the most vast empire owed their existence to
this monarch. Nor would be less surprising his portrait *if [when]* one would consider Trajan as man of
war. But the public virtues, *rather than [not indeed]* [36]
the military, were those which merited for him the
name of father of his country, and under this aspect
alone he is worthy of esteem and of admiration.

[1] non vi fu al. [2] dimestichezza, famigliarità. [3] ostentazione.
[4] contrassegno. [5] ingresso a piedi. [6] calca. [7] gli si affollava d'intorno.
[8] pure. [9] starsene per istrada. [10] gentile. [11] a diporto. [12] Bel
vedere portarsi. [13] cocchio, oppure. [14] brigata. [15] recarsi. [16] sedile,
gli andava incontro. [17] piccolo petulante. [18] quella tanta. [19] av-
vilimento. [20] a tutta forza. [21] unico. [22] conseguì. [23] da poco.
[24] colmo. [25] giunse. [26] qualsisia. [27] lesa maestà. [28] essa sola.
[29] tramasse insidie. [30] accomodare. [31] radere. [32] allegro. [33] con-
vitati. [34] impugnate. [35] gli argini. [36] non già.

[1] The use of the preterit here implies "*never was*"; the imperfect would mean "*was not then.*" [3] A more general term than
fasto, which is used chiefly of *worldly* pride and display. [7], [9], [16]
Parse. [14] A very usual word for *party* when it means *company on
a special occasion.* "La brigata andava pe' prati = the party
walked about the meadows." [23] Da poco, literally *fit for little,*
implies nullity and cowardice rather than moral evil. [24] Colmo
= brimfull. [27] Lesa is the past part. of ledere, to injure. [30] Note
the spelling; and remember that comodo, comando, comento comune,
cominciare, and all their derivatives, have but one m in Italian,
two in French and English. — Accomodare = to *settle* or *put
right,* must be translated according to the sense. Sometimes it
means to *mend:* "accomodatemi questo vestito, mend this coat for
me." Accomodarsi = to sit down: "favorisca accomodarsi, be so
kind as to sit down." — Accomodarsi di = to put up with, make
the best of: "bisognerà accomodarsi di quest' alloggio, we must
put up with this lodging." [34] From pugno = first: whence also
pugnale = poniard.

---

39. Antoninus Pius.

Antoninus, *surnamed* [1] the Pious, was born in Lanuvium the year 86 of the vulgar era. He was created Proconsul of Asia, then Governor of Italy, and
Consul at last, the year 120. In each of these eminent
posts he was always such as he *remained* [*preserved*

himself] on the first throne of the world, moderate, affable, wise, prudent, most just. He *began* [*gave beginning*] by the action most dear to his heart, that of diminishing the public *imposts*[2]: *he gave ear*[3] to the laments of any who complained of being too much *burdened*[4], nor tolerated that any should be oppressed for default of payment.

Economist of the substances of the subjects, he was, on the contrary, so liberal of his own, that in acts of beneficence he consumed his entire patrimony. On occasion of inundations, or of *dearths, he lavished*[5] all the succours which the circumstances demanded; if a disaster afflicted some city, he comforted it with his munificences: if any remained prey to the fire, he made it at once be rebuilt; thus it was *with* [*of*] Narbonne, with Antioch, with Rome and with several others, without *moreover*[6] speaking of many which he adorned with useful and magnificent monuments.

That which Antoninus feared more than all, was to *cause* [*bring*] a displeasure to his people; he could not *bear*[7] to cause an *annoyance*[8] even to his most declared enemies. Being-convicted certain wretches of having conspired against his life, he *forbade*[9] rigidly to the Senate to proceed against them. This Socrates on the throne protected likewise the liberty of the consciences and of the worships. He tolerated not that should be denounced as a crime the professing a religion diverse from that of the State, and although he was a pagan he *thundered*[10] penalties against the Gentiles who should dare accuse the Christians.

But that which placed Antoninus above sovereigns was the unspeakable care to *cause to be tasted* [*make taste*] constantly the fruits of peace *by* [*to*] his subjects, holding in check the enemies *by means of*[11] the mere respect and fear which his name impressed. So much reputation had the rectitude and the wisdom of his government procured to him, that some nations spontaneously rendered themselves tributary to him, others which had not before *any connexion [relation]* with him sent to him ambassadors, and others, finally, supplicated him to give them a sovereign at his choice. If by chance he heard *lavished [to lavish]* praises on those illustrious assassins who had desolated the earth with their conquests, he repeated the saying of Scipio Africanus: "As for me, I prefer the life of one citizen to the death of a thousand foes." Intent therefore to render happy the peoples, and not to *enlarge [dilate]* the empire at costs of their substances, he knew always to avoid war, without *injuring the reputation [offending the decorum]* of the nation and *thus it happened*[12] that the cities and the provinces were never so *flourishing [florid]*, as they were under him.

This model of kings, to whom no one imputed defects, neither as private-man, nor as prince, *filled his [covered the]* pacific throne twentythree years. His death was a true misfortune for the human kind.

[1] cognominato. [2] imposizioni. [3] porse orecchio. [4] aggravato. [5] carestie, profuse. [6] poi. [7] sostenere. [8] disgusto. [9] vietò. [10] fulminò. [11] mediante. [12] ne venne così.

[4] What adj. is the root? Shew the connexion with the Eng. *aggravate.* [5] The root of carestia? [8] Disgusto = dis-gusto = disgust = distaste. Used here differently from the English sense of either; but in Italian this meaning is common. Connect the two. [12] Parse.

40. Marcus Aurelius.

Dead the *adoptive*[1] father Antoninus Pius, was of unanimous consent proclaimed Emperor his son Marcus Aurelius Antoninus, who, although alone called to the throne, nevertheless divided the power and the honours with Lucius Verus his brother, and this because he also had been adopted by his admirable predecessor.

Marcus Aurelius, born, to so say, philosopher, had even from the age of twelve years embraced a *kind*[2] of life sober and austere. His bed was the bare ground, and it was only to obey his mother that he substituted for it a mattress. The only scope of all his actions was the acquisition of the moral virtues.

Mounted on the throne, he commenced from the project to *shelter* [*cover*] for ever the felicity of the people from the blows of despotism, raising again the *downcast*[3] authority of the senate. He assisted at the assemblies of this body with the assiduity of the *lowest* [*last*] candidate, and when several were of an opinion contrary to his, he preferred *the others' view*[4], saying: "It is more reasonable to follow the opinion of several sages, than to oblige them to bow themselves to that of one only." If *he was in need*[5] of something, he asked it religiously *from*[6] the Senate, *in*[6] whose presence, not less than in that of the people, not *seldom*[7] he was accustomed to say: "Romans, I have nothing of *my own* [*mine*]: the very house that I inhabit is your *property*[8] "

In the execution he avoided *alike*[9] slowness and precipitation, loving very much to be exact, because he was of *opinion*[10] that the *neglecting*[11] the little evil was an opening the *way*[12] to the great. In the choice of the governors, of the magistrates, of the judges, he used much circumspection, accustomed to say that "a Prince cannot indeed create the men *such as*[13] he would that they should be, but can nevertheless *make use of them according to* [*apply them in tenor of*] their capacity." Nor did he repute himself *any* [*other*] thing except a minister of the state equally with the others, and so much subordinate to the law, that one day, in the ceremony of conferring the sword on a *prefect of the prætorium*[14], he addressed to him these memorable words: "I consign it to you, in order that you use it in my defence, *as long as*[15] I shall do my duty: you will turn it against me, if I shall forget the *good* [*felicity*] of the Romans."

Such conduct had excited in his favour the enthusiasm of the subjects: they regarded him no more as a man, but as a god; the senate wanted at every cost to raise to him temples and altars. Marcus Aurelius heard this with a species of horror, nor suffered such *sacrilegious*[16] effusions of heart. "*Virtue alone* [*The only virtue*]," he said, "equals men to the Gods, and this is *incontestable*[17]; but a just king has the universe for temple, and *good men*[18] are his *priests*[19]."

If to raise to the most eminent grade his virtues nothing had been wanting to him but *misfortunes*[20], he sustained of them very many. He saw *vexed*[21] his empire by grave and numerous calamities, and strongly threatened by the barbarians. In such *difficulties*[22], it was his great care to lighten *as far as possible* [*possibly*] on the back of the subjects the public burdens, in their stead loading with them his. Statues, *pictures*[23], furniture of the *palace*[24], pearls, precious stones, all the gold, all the silver that he had, even to the ornaments and the garments of the empress herself, everything was by him distributed or sold, *so that*[25] the subjects might not be too much *burdened* [*aggravated*].

Being-driven out and repressed the enemies, he applied himself to reform the laws, to protect the *fate*[26] of orphans and of minors, to fortify the subjects against the *legal frauds*[27], to curb luxury and general dissoluteness. Having-passed then into Athens, he founded *chairs*[28] of sciences, elected professors, assigned to them stipends and accorded immunities: on his return to Rome, he condoned to each debtor the sum due to the *treasury*[29], burning in public the documents that authenticated the debt; and that same who had always refused every honour for himself, *caused to be raised* [*made raise*] statues to those brave men who had signalized themselves under his orders.

In his reposes of Lanuvium he threw himself *into the arms of*[30] philosophy, which he called his mother, in opposition to the court, which he *called* [*said*] his stepmother. There he applied himself to compose the Reflections upon himself, one of the most pure *codes*[31] of morals which antiquity *has*[32] transmitted to us; there he repeated often that platonic[33] saying: "Happy the kingdoms in which the kings are philosophers, and in which the philosophers are kings!"

He died *on*[34] journey marching against a new incursion of barbarians, after nineteen years of empire, in the fiftyninth of his age.

[1]adottivo. [2]genere. [3]abbattuta. [4]l'altrui parere. [5]abbisognava. [6]a. [7]di rado. [8]roba. [9]del pari. [10]avviso. [11]trascurare. [12]adito. [13]quali. [14]prefetto del pretorio. [15]finchè. [16]sacrileghe. [17]incontrastabile. [18]galantuomini. [19]sacerdoti [20]sciagure. [21]tra-

vagliato. ²²frangenti. ²³ quadri. ²⁴reggia. ²⁵purche. ²⁶sorte.
²⁷insidie forensi. ²⁸cattedre. ²⁹erario. ³⁰in braccio alla. ³¹codici.
³²abbia. ³³platonico. ³⁴per.

¹Adj. ⁵Abbisognare di = aver bisogno di. ⁷Rado = raro.
⁸A noun of multitude, signifying *things, property* in general, and always used in the singular. "Levate di qui tutta questa roba, take away all these things, all this litter." ¹³Tali is understood before quali. The first term in comparisons of equality is frequently omitted. ²¹Remember that travagliare does not correspond to the Fr. *travailler.* ²³Quadro = picture: pittura = art of painting. "Questo signore esercita la pittura, ed ha fatto un bel quadro = this gentleman's profession is painting and he has executed a fine picture." ²⁴Used only of a *sovereign's* palace; whereas palazzo is also used of a nobleman's mansion, if sufficiently splendid. ²⁷Forense is from Foro, as trials took place in the *Forum;* whence also our *forensic.* ³²The subjunctive is used after a superlative.

41. Publius Ælius Pertinax.

Let there be read that which Publius Ælius Pertinax *was able* [*knew*] to do in eighty-seven days of reign. Raised to the imperial throne, the year 193, he set himself at once to repress the *arrogance* [*petulance*] of the prætorian guard, *obnoxious* [*troublesome*]¹ to every class of citizens; he banished the informers, and reformed many abuses introduced *newly*² in the exercise of justice. *He caused to be sold by auction*³, as if they were slaves, all the buffoons and the *jesters*⁴ who had served *as pastime to*⁵ Commodus, and who had rendered themselves infamous by their conduct, and he exposed also to sale *real and personal property*⁶ of this his wicked predecessor which had fallen into his *ownership* [*property*], assigning of them *the pro-*

ceeds[7] to the treasury, whereby to lighten the imposts, and *causing to be restored* [*making render*] to the private persons all that which that plunderer had usurped from them. He abolished also the *tolls*[8] established at the *entrance* [*ingress*] of the bridges, at the passage of the rivers, at the *passage along* [*transit of*] the roads, which *clogged*[9] the public liberty. He let the barren *lands* [*goods*] of the crown, exempting for ten years the cultivators of them from the *rural*[10] tax, and assuring them that, *during his life*[11], they *would not be, on this account, molested with lawsuits* [*would not have been, on this article, molested in judgment*]; nor *suffered* [*tolerated*] he that should be placed his name on the *entrance* [*ingress*] to those places which were of *the imperial domain* [*imperial dominion*], saying that they belonged not to him, but to the empire. He reduced *by one half* [*to the only half*] the ordinary expences of his palace; and because the Emperor adopted the frugality of the table, this became at once in Rome an affair of fashion, *so that provisions abated suddenly*[12] of price. Pertinax *suffered* [*had*] the unmerited and *untimely* [*unripe*] fate of Probus, emperors assassinated by the military whom they wanted to oblige to the duty.

[1] infesti. [2] di nuovo. [3] fece porre all' incanto. [4] giocolari. [5] a trastullo di. [6] fondi e mobili. [7] il ritratto. [8] gravezze. [9] inceppavano. [10] prediale. [11] sua vita durante. [12] in guisa che i viveri ribassarono repentemente.

[3], [12] Parse. [7] Ritrarre da = to draw from. [12] Viveri = victuals. — Repente = sudden. Never confuse it with the Eng. *repent.*

42. Marcus Claudius Tacitus.

Marcus Claudius Tacitus, in six only months of empire, pushed *so far*[1] the beneficent profusions, that, instead of profiting by the public revenues, he sacrificed to the good of the State seven *to* [*in*] eight millions of gold which he possessed, as much in personal as in real property. He willed that justice, exempt from corruption, should be administered indiscriminately to whomsoever, and published to such end *most holy*[2] laws. There was no emperor who accorded to the senate greater authority; *he regulated himself always by*[3] its counsels, and so much respected it, that having requested of it the consulate for his brother, having received from it the repulse, he opened not mouth except to say: "We must believe that it can make a better choice."

Enemy of luxury, he never suffered that the Empress his wife should adorn herself with precious stones, and to whomsoever he prohibited the use of dresses with gold embroidery. He re-established *morality*[4], because he was the first to give of it the example.

[1] tant' oltre. [2] santissime. [3] reggeasi sempre a norma de'. [4] il costume.

[2] This word is often applied to laws and justice. [3] Parse.

43. Valentinian II.

The life of Valentinian II is a prodigy, *when one considers*[1] that this emperor, although a youth, wisely reigned from the years thirteen to the twenty of his age, when others need to be *ruled*[2], having-remained afterwards victim of the cruel ambition of a *rival*[3], for *supreme*[4] misfortune of the peoples to him subject. On the throne he was *master of himself, a kind of rule [the hero of himself, quality of enterprize]* so much the more glorious, as it is the more of rare and *difficult attainment*[5].

When it reached his ear that he was a youth too much *addicted*[6] to the games of the circus, he abolished those even which were customary on the day of the birth of the sovereign; when, in fine, he knew that some blamed him because willingly he assisted at the public combats of the *wild beasts*[7], *he immediately had killed [made immediately kill]* those which were destined to such use. No one is more *fit [apt]* to reign than he who knows thus to reign over himself.

It happened that the principals of a distinguished family were accused of having plotted against his days. He *removed*[8] this affair to his immediate jurisdiction, and in examining the proofs, *which were but too evident [even too speaking]*, he knew with such clemency to weaken their force, that *the accused appeared*[9] not guilty. He *dismissed*[10] them with the memorable words: "I must trust you: *mistrust [diffidence] torments none but*[11] tyrants."

A youth wholly intent, not on enjoying himself, not on building himself[12] a false glory, but *on being [to be]* father to his people, he lightened extremely the imposts, resisting opposite counsels. "How ever," he said, "*should there be imposed*[13] new burdens on those who *scàrcely can with difficulty*[14] pay the old?" His great reward was the pleasure of seeing the sensible effects of his just and moderate government: *abundance and peace.*

¹allorchè si consideri. ²dominati. ³emulo. ⁴somma. ⁵malagevole riuscimento. ⁶propenso. ⁷fiere. ⁸avocò. ⁹gl'imputati comparvero. ¹⁰licenziò. ¹¹non tormenta fuorchè. ¹²giovane tutto occupato, non a darsi bel tempo, non a fabbricarsi. ¹³hanno ad imporsi. ¹⁴appena possono a stento.

¹Allorchè and quando, when used for se, govern the subjunctive. ³From the same root as our —? Trace the connexion. ⁴Rather than supremo in speaking of evils. ⁵Agevole = facile; malagevole = difficile. ⁶Like our —? ⁸A law term. ¹⁰Dar licenza = to give leave: prender licenza = licenziarsi = to take leave; licenziare = to dismiss = to give leave (or command) to depart. ¹²Parse; and note the prep. required by occupato before an infin., and the idiom darsi bel tempo. ¹³Note this idiomatic use of avere a, which must be rendered as above. But with da as in English: "*ho* da andarci I *have* to go there." ¹⁴A forcible and allowable tautology.

44. Peter the Great.

The *Czar*¹ Peter the Great, in fifty-three years of life, to *polish*² his nation worked such prodigies, that he alone carried it to that grade of civilization to which, without him, it would scarcely have attained in three centuries. Legislation, policy, military and civil discipline, marine, commerce, sciences, fine arts, manufactures, all was born, grew and in part also was perfected *by his means* [*through his work*] in the central *spots*³ at least of his most vast empire.

Let a rapid glance be thrown over *only the* [*the only*] principal establishments *for* [*of*] which Russia

7*

is indebted [*goes debtor*] to this great genius. He set on foot an infantry of hundred thousand soldiers, so fine and so *warlike*[4], that other was there not then in Europe which surpassed it, and he gave being to a *navy*[5] of forty vessels of the line and of four hundred galleys. All the fortresses which deserved it were girt with walls according to the last prescriptions of the art, and he admirably disciplined the great cities which were *previously*[6] as dangerous, *by* [*the*] night, as the most remote *forests*[7].

An academy of marine and of *navigation*[8], to which all the noble families *were bound*[9] to send a son; colleges of mathematics, of languages, of polite literature at Moscow, at Petersburg, at Kiow; elementary schools sown through all the villages, are of the number of his precious establishments. Be there added a college of medicine and a great *druggery*[10] at Moscow, *to supply*[11] remedies to the principal cities and to the *forces*[12], when *before*[6] in all the empire there was not even one *druggist*[13], and, if those of the Czar are excepted, not even a single physician: public *lectures on* [*lessons of*] anatomy, of which was ignored even the name, and that which might *be estimated*[14] as a *standing* [*perpetual*] lecture, the celebrated anatomical cabinet of Ruisch, *bought* [*acquired*] by the Emperor in Holland and sent to Petersburg; *besides yet*[15] an observatory, in which the astronomers began to occupy themselves *with* [*in*] the study of the heaven, and a most rich cabinet which contained the most *various*[16] and curious productions of nature.

It was also his merit the introduction of new *printing-presses*[17] with reformed alphabetical letters, and *the substitution for* [*to*] *the barbarous abbreviations*[18] of characters *easily read* [*of easy intelligence*], by which books ceased at last to be in Russia more rare than *any foreign merchandize*[19] He established interpreters for all the languages of Europe and Asia, *including even*[20] Chinese, *and especially of course*[21] for those of the learned, Latin and Greek; and he founded a royal *library*[22] composed of the three very rich ones which he had bought in England, in the Holstein and in Germany.

The architecture which *was used*[23] in Russia was of the most *clumsy*[24] and deformed; he *refined*[25] it to our usage, and buildings appeared commodious and regular, *seemly*[26] palaces and public edifices; and the many other arts which he transplanted with his own hand into countries almost all savage, seem at the *present day* [*day of today*] natural to those regions. Geography is *debtor*[27] to him above all, *witness*[28] the discoveries, made under his auspices, around the Caspian Sea, of whose *circumference* [*circuit*] gave he the first to Europe a most exact chart.

Surmounting obstacles insuperable to *any* [*every*] soul less energetic than his, persuaded that where ignorance and error dominate, it is needful to do men good by force, he *extended* [*pushed*] the *polishing*[29] of his subjects even to the clothes and to the aspect of the person. He created his own nation: it seemed that the genius to *refine*[2], to civilize *he must have received from above*[30], and it were in him a celestial inspiration.

[1] The same. [2] dirozzare. [3] punti. [4] agguerrita. [5] marina. [6] prima. [7] boscaglie. [8] nautica. [9] doveano. [10] spezieria. [11] per somministrare. [12] armate. [13] speziale. [14] valutarsi. [15] oltre poi

ad. [16]svariate. [17]stamperie. [18]"The substitution" must come *after* "abbreviations." [19]qualsisia merce straniera. [20]compresa la stessa. [21]non che. [22]biblioteca. [23]costumavasi. [24]grossolane. [25]ingentill. [26]decorosi. [27]debitrice. [28]attese. [29]ripulimento. [30]lo tenesse dall' alto.

[2]Rozzo = rough, rustic. [6]Indeclinable, of course, because it is what part of speech? It is also —? [11]*Per* expresses a much more definite surpose than a; use it whenever *in order to* would be admissible in English. [12]This will include land and sea forces. When both are not included, esercito is preferable for *army*, though armata is also used; but the strict sense of this latter word is *fleet*; like our *armament*, and the Spanish armada. [18]Can you account for this inversion? I wish the same were possible in English; it places *the substitution* in proximity with *of characters*, and so avoids ambiguity and looseness of construction. [19]Analyse qualsisia. [20], [30]Parse. [21]No English term will so represent non che as to preserve at once the sense and the construction, and void awkward prepositions; "not to speak of" is usually the best; but the Irish idiom *let alone* comes nearer. "Egli parla bene l'italiano e lo spagnuolo, non che il francese = he speaks Italian and Spanish well, *not to speak of (let alone)* French." [22]Biblioteca and libreria differ as their French equivalents: the first is *library*, the second *bookshop* or *circulating library*. [27]Why not debitore? [28]The pass. part. of attendere; no literal rendering is possible.

45. Disinterestedness of Charles XII.

Charles XII, the Swedish Rodomont, was walking *not far [little distant]* from Leipsic, when a peasant threw himself at his feet, and begged of him justice against a *grenadier*[1] who had snatched the dinner from his family. The King made soon come to him the accused, and *roughly*[2] interrogated him if *the robbery were true* [*were true the rapine*] that *was* [*came*] imputed to him. "Sire," answered this-man, "I have not *after all*[3] done so much harm to this peasant, as you have done to his master: your Majesty has despoiled him of a kingdom, and I after all have not *taken*[4] from this man *more than* [*except*] a fowl." Charles, imperturbable at such bold words, turned to the peasant and *counted out* [*numbered*] to him ten ducats; then calm answered to the grenadier: "Remember, my friend, that if I have *taken away*[4] a kingdom from the king Augustus, I have not reserved anything for myself."

[1]granatiere. [2]bruscamente. [3]poi. [4]tolto.

46. Love of the Subjects preferred to the paternal.

John II, King of Portugal, called the *Great* and the *Severe*, encountered the misfortune to lose an only son whom he loved tenderly, although he had not corresponded to the efforts made by him to educate him. When there was brought to him the news of it, he said thing than which none more magnanimous and more affectionate issued ever from the mouth of any Sovereign: "That which consoles me is, that this boy was not adapted to reign, and that God by taking him from me has made *known* [*know*] how much He protects my people."

47. Frederick II.

The night which followed the battle of Torgau was very cold, and the victorious Prussian troops passed

it under arms, beside a multitude of fires. At the
dawn[1] of the new day, the King Frederick, who had
commanded the left wing, *transferred* [*transported*]
himself to the right, and being-arrived where *was*
[*found itself*] the regiment of his foot-guards, having-
dismounted from horseback, seated himself at the fire,
surrounded by the grenadiers who awaited the new
day to resume the attack, *in case* [*when*] the Austrians
should not have taken the *course*[2] to abandon the field
of battle.

Several of them were crowded around him; he was
talking familiarly with all, and was praising that regiment which had comported itself with much valour;
when behold one of these grenadiers, called Rubiack,
whom Frederick had rewarded several times, spoke to
him in this guise: "Where wast thou at the moment
of the battle? we are accustomed to see thee always
at our head, and to be led by thee into the *thickest*
[*strongest*] of the *fray*[3]; today however thou hast not
shewn[4] thyself: it is not good thing that thou abandon
us thus." The great man, *accustomed*[5] already to this
style, as if to exculpate himself, placidly answered,
that having commanded the left wing, he had not
therefore been able to find himself in their company.

Continuing this military conversation, the excessive
heat began to incommode the monarch who, to *cool
himself*[6], unbuttoned his great-coat, from which the
soldiers saw drop a ball which had *pierced*[7] his *order*
[*device*]. *Seized*[8] by enthusiasm, at such sight, they
set themselves *with one voice* [*of accord*] to cry: "Yes,
thou art indeed [*that thou art*] our ancient little-
Frederick[9]; yes, *thou dost indeed share* [*that thou
dividest*] always the dangers with us: we will die

willingly for thee: live the King! live Frederick! *up comrades*[10], at the Austrians! at the Austrians! let us march, let us advance!" In the twinkling of an eye they dispose themselves in line, nor *is it easy* [*little needs there*][11] for the officers to restrain that ardour, and to make *them*[12] comprehend that not yet is arrived the moment to renew the *fight*[13].

[1] alba. [2] partito. [3] mischia. [4] fatto vedere. [5] assuefatto. [6] rinfrescarsi. [7] forato. [8] còlti. [9] Federighetto. [10] orsù compagni. [11] poco ci vuole. [12] loro. [13] pugna.

[3] The French *mêlée*. [4] A very usual expression. — "Fammi vedere il tuo nuovo libro = shew me your new book." [6] Fresco has more the sense of *cold* than our *fresh* has. — It is highly idiomatic in this phrase: "stai fresco = it is all over with you." [7] Forare = to pierce or drill with holes. Traforare = to embroider in open-work (Fr. *broder a jour*). [12] Fare here governs the infin. and the infin. the conjunctive pronoun in the dative case. (How do you know loro to be here a conj. pron.?) The cases connected with fare and an infin. require, as in French, careful consideration. Parse these phrases: — fateglielo dire — fatelo passare — me lo fece scrivere — gli farò leggere quella storia — le farai dare una limosina — bisogna farlo castigare: — and account for the cases.

48. HUMANITY OF THE EMPEROR FRANCIS I.

In the inundation of the Danube of the year 1747, one of the suburbs of Vienna ran the most *serious*[1] risk. The houses *half*[2] submerged and struck by the *blocks* [*slabs*][3] of ice and by the *fragments*[4] of other edifices precipitously descending, threatened to *fall*[5], and the inhabitants, on the roofs, their hands raised to heaven, demanded *with*[6] loud cries succour. The Emperor Francis, husband of Maria Theresa, *hastened himself*[7] near to the river, *to*[6] animate the boatmen with the most intense fervour, *in order that*[8] they should lend aid to those unhappy ones; but the fear to perish was such in all that no one *could bring himself* [*would induce himself*] to this heroic resolution. The obstacles which intimidated the others, could not however keep back longer the Sovereign; he jumped into a boat, saying: "I hope that at seeing me set off the first, you will resolve afterwards to follow me." The magnanimous example delayed not to be imitated; and as many as were *about*[9] to lose the life, were conducted to *safety*[10].

[1]grave. [2]per metà. [3]lastre. [4]rottami. [5]crollare. [6]ad.
[7]accorse egli stesso. [8]affinchè. [9]in procinto. [10]salvezza.

[3]From the same root as our lastricate [4]From rompere, rotto.
[6]After verbs of motion *a* is often more idiomatic than *per* to express a definite purpose. [7]The Fr. *accourut.* [8]*Per* = in order to; governs the infin. Affinchè = a fin che = to the end that = in order that; governs the subj. Note in this word and many others the application of the rule that when two words, the first ending in a vowel, the second beginning with a consonant, are joined in one, the consonant with which the second begins is doubled.

---

49. Visit of Maria Theresa.

Maria Theresa, finding herself at Luxemburg, *received*[1] a messenger sent [*directed*] to her by a woman of a hundred and eight years, who for a long

tract of time had not ever failed to *be* [*find herself*] in
the number of the *poor*[2] whose feet Her Majesty
washed *on* [*the*] Holy Thursday. She *sent word* [*made
say*] to the Empress, that she *experienced* [*proved*] the
most lively *regret at seeing herself, on account of her
infirmities, deprived for two years past of the power*[3]
to assist at this pious ceremony, not *indeed*[4] for the
ceremony, not indeed for the loss of the honour that
to [*in*] her came from it, but because *she was unable*[5]
any more to see a sovereign whom she adored.

The empress *moved*[6] by the sentiment of that good
woman, did not disdain to repair to her village and
to enter into her *cottage*[7]. She found her stretched in
a little bed, kept there by the infirmities companions
inseparable of decrepitude. "*You complain*[8] of not
having been able to see me," says to her with kindness
this generous Sovereign; "console yourself, good little-
old-woman; it is I that come to see you." Who could
describe what effect produces on the heart of this poor
woman the presence of her empress, and the consoling
words that she *addressed* [*directed*] to her? Her eyes
were bathed in tears, her mouth half-open could not
articulate word; she stretched her hands *clasped*[9] and
trembling towards the Princess, whom she regarded
as[10] angel descended from heaven to console her in
her troubles. Maria Theresa *affected*[11] by the *baffled
longings of this poor woman* [*violence experienced by
this miserable*], who groaned not to be able to get out
from the bed to throw herself at her feet, stayed long
in her company, and on retiring left to her a generous
alms[12]. She who had a heart made for such visits,
must have certainly felt[13] for her subjects the affection
of mother.

¹accolse. ²povere. ³dispiacere nel vedersi, attese le sue in-
fermità, tolto da due anni il potere. ⁴già. ⁵le era conteso.
⁶commossa. ⁷tugurio. ⁸vi dolete. ⁹giunte. ¹⁰qual. ¹¹intenerita.
¹²sovvenimento. ¹³dovea sentire al certo.

³Parse, and attend most carefully to the cases. — Vedere has
for its direct complement the clause tolto il potere. — Recall a
former note on atteso. — Da due anni = for 2 years past, and
still. Due anni fa = 2 years ago. ⁵Literally "it was contended
= disputed = hindered to her." ⁶Muovere = to move materially;
commuovere = to move mentally. There is a corresponding difference between our *motion* and *emotion.* ⁷Perhaps *hut;* a word
belonging to the noble style. Cottage is usually capanna. ⁸Dolersi
= to *complain* as a sufferer: lagnarsi = to *complain* as an
aggrieved person. ¹⁰Quale is equivalent to *as* when the possession
of certain *qualities* (qualità being from the same root) is implied;
as here. ¹¹From tenero, adj. Intenerire and commuovere are
synonyms. ¹²More literally *aid.* ¹³Parse, and account for the
tense of dovere.

50. Joseph II.

Of these visits there made several also Joseph II,
her son. One day he repaired to the house of a poor
*soldier*¹, and surprised him when he sat at table, surrounded by eleven children. "I knew," said he, "that
you had ten of them; but who is that eleventh that I
see there?" — "Sire," rejoined the officer, "he is a
poor little orphan whom I have found exposed *at*² the
door of my house, *nor did my feelings allow me*³ to
abandon him." — "I will," resumed then the Emperor,
moved by such action, "that all these children be my
pensioners, and continue you to give them examples of
honour and of virtue. I will pay to each two hundred

florins a[4] year, and tomorrow you will come to *draw*[5] the first quarter of it."

Another day, his carriage having [6] *stopped* [*suspended the course*] in a street of Vienna, there presented himself to him a boy of about nine years, who *began* [*set himself*] to speak to him thus: "Sire, I have never begged, but my mother is dying. In order to have a physician *I want* [*there needs to me*] a florin, and we have not one. Ah! if Your Majesty would present to me one of them, I could *recover*[7] my mother, and we then *should be happy*[8]."

The Emperor asked him of the name and of the habitation of the invalid, and having had [*of it*] the answer, gave him the florin. The child, who had bent the knee to earth, rose up again and *began* [*set himself*] to run without even thanking him.

Then the Sovereign descends *on a sudden from*[9] carriage, wraps himself in his mantle; and followed by *one of his servants, hurries*[10] to house of the sick woman, who takes him for the physician, describes to him her *ailment*[11] and begs him to prescribe for her some thing which *may avail*[12] to cure her. The Monarch, *representing* [*represented*] that personage who availed best to keep the *poor woman under her mistake* [*miserable in the illusion*], makes use of *her son's inkstand* [*an inkstand of the son*] wherewith to write a *prescription* [*receipt*], gives her courage and departs.

Scarcely was he gone [*Gone he scarcely*], *came up*[13] the boy with his florin, in company of the true physician. The woman astonished informed him that she had already been visited by another, who even had left to her a *prescription*[14]. The doctor setting himself to read it, recognised the handwriting and the *signature*[15] of the sovereign; he deciphered to her the mystery, *acquainting her* [16] that that paper *contained nothing* else than [17] an assignment of a hundred florins, *charged* [18] on the properties of the sovereign himself, and it was remedy perhaps for her the most salutary of all.

[1]militare. [2]su. [3]mi diede l'animo. [4]all'. [5]riscuotere. [6]Consult the former note on the position of the gerund. [7]ricuperare. [8]staremmo bene. [9]in un subito di. [10]uno de' suoi, si porta frettoloso. [11]male. [12]valga. [13]sopraggiunse. [14]ordinazione. [15]soscrizione. [16]partecipandole. [17]non altro contenea che. [18]caricata.

[1]A more dignified term than soldato, which would not be used of an officer. [3]Parse. — Anima = the soul in general, and especially as the principle of life. Animo = the soul as the seat of mind, thought, passion, settled purpose. With the first connect our *animate;* with the second *animosity.* [8]Star bene, usually = to be well in health, must sometimes be translated *to be comfortable, happy, well off.* [10]I miei, i tuoi, i suoi, &c. may be used without a noun of kindred in general, and of the various inferior relations of life, and must be translated according to the sense. Used by or of a *father,* they will be equivalent to his *family,* his *children;* in the case of a *master,* to his *servants;* of a *king,* to his *attendants,* &c.; of a *general,* to his *soldiers;* and so on. — "I miei salutano caramente i tuoi, my family send their love to yours." "Il capitano corse all' assalto alla testa de' suoi, the captain rushed to the attack at the head of his regiment." [11]A general term, not necessarily as strong as malattia. [15]Soscrizione = sotto scrizione = subscription = under-writing = signature.

51. The pretended Mediator.

Another day, the same Emperor *was strolling about* [1] Vienna, *in* [to] manner of any other private person, when *he met with* [2] a young woman, *most sad* [3] in

countenance, who carried under her arm a heavy bundle.
"Where go you?" he said to her graciously, following
her: "Could not I soften the grief by which you appear to me pierced?" — "I carry to sell, sir, *some
household goods*⁴ which belong to my poor mother,"
and, *while some tears trickled*⁵, added: "These, see,
are the last utensils which remain to us. Ah! if my
father, who was a brave officer, lived still, or if he
had at least obtained for his family the recompence that
he merited, we should not be *indeed*⁶ in this state." —
"But if such circumstances," resumed the unknown,
"were known to the Emperor, *by this time* [*today*] you
would certainly not have *aught whereof* [*of what*] to
complain: he loves justice and beneficence. Present to
him a memorial, or charge some one that he expose
to him your wants." — "I have done it, sir, but
uselessly. The person to whom we have recommended
ourselves has made us understand *that he has not*
[*not to have*] been able to succeed in it." — "*Lies
have been told you* [*To you have been told lies*], you
were deceived, poor women," resumed the Sovereign,
ill *repressing*⁷ the pain which caused to him such a
discourse; "I can assure you that *there cannot have
reached him*⁸ the least notice of all this; he has never
let perish widows and daughters of officers who have
done their duty. *Come*⁹, listen to me; at nine in the
morning I will *be* [*find myself*] tomorrow at the entrance of the imperial palace; bring me your *petitions*¹⁰
in writing, and if *what*¹¹ you say is the truth, it will
be my *business*¹² to make you speak to the Emperor,
and from him you will have justice."

The young woman, *drying*¹³ her tears, lavished
thanks on the unknown, when the latter added: "It *is*

[*goes*] not well, meanwhile, good girl, that you should sell these utensils. How much think you to be able to *obtain*[14] for them?" — "Sir .... I should think .... ten florins." — "Well, permit me that I lend you twenty of them; you will return them to me when my *negociations*[15] shall have *achieved*[16] some good *success* [*issue*][17]. Run to *comfort*[18] your mother: *farewell till* [*to see each other again*][19] tomorrow."

Stunned the young woman and agitated by a hundred affections, returned home with her bundle and the received money, nor was she ever satiated *with repeating* [*to repeat*] to her mother and to the bystanders the most minute circumstances of this adventure. Some, in hearing her however *describe so vividly* [*speak so to the life*][20], recognised evidently in that unknown the Emperor, who *indeed*[6] used to make such sweet surprises. Fell then the daughter into the greatest disturbance, fearing to have spoken too freely to her prince, and *trembled at having* [*palpitated to have*] to repair the day following to his presence; but her relations *encouraged*[18] her; they promised to accompany her, and she at last *took* [*made herself*] heart and went there.

When she saw him, she recognised at once in the benefactor the Monarch; there came to her a *trembling*[21] and surprised her a *swoon*[22] The Emperor had already assured himself that she had said to him nought but the truth, and when she regained the use of her senses, he introduced her into a *room*[23] and said to her: "Here is for your mother the rescript of a pension equivalent to the pay that your father had, the half of which will be enjoyed by you, if you shall have the misfortune to lose her. It grieves me not to have known sooner your lot; I would not have tolerated that you should have encountered it." — This is to love one's [the] subjects in earnest[24].

[1]girava per. [2]si abbattè in. [3]mestissima. [4]alcune masserizie. [5]scendendole qualche lagrima. [6]già. [7]comprimendo. [8]non gli sarà pervenuta. [9]orsù. [10]ricerche. [11]quanto. [12]impegno. [13]tergendo. [14]ritrarre. [15]maneggi. [16]riportato. [17]esito. [18]confortare, confortarono. [19]a rivederci. [20]life, vivo. [21]tremito. [22]deliquio. [23]stanza. [24]daddovero.

[4]Why not "delle masserizie"? Because del, &c. is the partitive article, and as such is used for some = a part or portion of the whole; thus "datemi del pane = datemi una porzione del pane ch'è sulla tavola, ecc. = give me some bread." But some is not here used in a partitive sense as meaning part of a stock of utensils; it means "certain utensils," therefore the pronoun alcune is preferred. As a rule you should render some otherwise than by the part. art., when certain could be substituted in English. In French there is the same distinction between du, &c. and quelque. [8]The future tense is idiomatically used to express a conjecture or conclusion. — "Ciò sarà = that may be." — "Avrete ragione = you may be right." — "Non l'avrà detto = he cannot have said it, most likely he did not say it." — "Vedrete che non l'avrà fatto = you will be sure to find he never did it." [12]Impegnarsi (from pegno, pledge) to engage; but impegno cannot always be rendered engagement; sometimes it is as here, my care, my business. [15]Maneggiare, maneggio, like their Fr. equivalents, must be rendered according to the sense. They come from mano, and the general idea is of something brought about without the person appearing whose hand is really in it. Maneggi is often contrivances. [18]The root is forte; and the idea (as in older English also) is of strengthening, encouraging, reviving hope. Consolare is the proper word when this is not the leading idea. [19]"A rivederci" is at least as usual as "addio" in ordinary leave-taking. [20]What part of speech?

8

NB. Henceforward such idioms only will be given word for word as have hitherto occurred rarely or not at all. — Occasionally, but by no means always, an italicized English word will be used to suggest that the rendering must be not literal, but idiomatic. — The object of this system — it cannot be too often repeated — is not to save pupils trouble; but to secure the full fruit of their trouble by preserving them from ever writing — and thus preserving their ear from ever becoming accustomed to — unidiomatic Italian.

52. The efficacious Recommendation[1].

A noble Neapolitan youth, not being able in his own country to obtain a military grade to his liking, determined, in the year 1774, to *go* [*carry himself*] to serve the emperor of Austria, to which effect he procured himself sundry recommendations, and *set out on his journey towards*[2] Vienna. Arrived at Grätz, he found in an inn three foreigners, in whose company he asked to sup; they were Germans, but all speaking French, he *became so familiar* [*familiarized himself so*] with them that he *imparted to them* his project. *When they had heard it* [*heard that they had it*[3]] one of them *began* [*took*] to speak to him thus: "Excuse me, but I am of opinion that you have taken a bad course. After a long peace, and in *the face* [*front*] of a prodigious number of noble youths who are asking employment, I see no *probability* [*appearance*] that a foreigner should *meet with* [*be able to find*] an officer's post in the army." — "Who knows?" answered the Neapolitan: "Meanwhile I *yield*[4] not to any in good will and in the desire which I have to distinguish myself. Besides I am furnished with let-

ters consigned to me by very *respectable*[5] persons,
and in spite of all the obstacles, I also think of trying
my fate."

The German who had *talked*[6] with him added:
"Since you *will have it* thus, I also should be *able*
[*in the case*] to do you a pleasure; I could, *if you
like*[7], furnish you with a letter which perhaps would
not *prove* [*turn out*] useless to you; I will recommend
you to the General Lascy, and you will present it in
person." The Neapolitan, full of gratitude, welcomed
the offer, and continued his journey.

Arrived in Vienna, he *distributed* [*diffused*] his recommendations; and as he had more than one for the
General, he failed not to present some to him also,
not including [*excepted*] however that of the German
traveller, which he had *mislaid*[8]. Lascy having read
them, *expressed* [*imparted*] to him his regret not to be
able, at least at that moment, to be useful to him,
attributing it to [*accusing thereof the*] circumstances.
The youth, who was already prepared for this, renounced
not his project, and hoping well for the future,
began to *pay* [*make*] his court to the General, by
whom he was always received with a barren politeness.

At last *it happened*[9] that he found again by chance
the letter that he thought lost. He delayed not to
present also this, not *concealing the casual encounter
through* [*dissimulating the combination by*][10] which he
had received it. Lascy opens it, *looks through it,
starts and hesitates*[11]. He asks of the Neapolitan, if he
knew the person who had consigned it to him. "No,
General," answers the youth. — "Well, my *friend*
[*dear*]", "the General resumes," you have had it from
the very hands of the Emperor. You would have

desired to be *second-lieutenant*[12], but he commands
me to make you first-lieutenant: you are so from this
moment; *be it now your part to fulfil your duty towards him [you will do afterwards towards him your
duty]*."

[1]commendatizia. [2]si pose in viaggio alla volta di. [4]la cedo.
[5]ragguardevoli. [6]ragionato. [7]se vi aggrada. [8]smarrita. [9]successe.
[11]la scorre, si scuote e resta sospeso. [12]sotto-tenente.

[3]The preterit, not the imperfect, of the auxiliary is always
used in clauses thus constructed. This construction is specially
idiomatic; pay great attention to it, and use it in your compositions.
[4]The la is expletive and idiomatic: a very frequent form. [6]Ragio-
nare = to reason, is also and much oftener = to discourse.
[10]Combinazione is also often our *coincidence.* [11]Sospeso = suspended = in suspense. But *hesitates* is here the best rendering
for resta sospeso.

53. Unfaithfulness condoned and prevented.

In the year 1765, an *official*[1] in the public *treasury*[2] of Sain-Polten had been shut up in prison for
having thence subtracted six hundred florins, his trial
was terminated, and *he was about to be condemned
[already one was about to condemn him].* Joseph II,
he of whom one would never cease to speak, was informed of this crime and of its circumstances; he
learned [knew][3] that the criminal, *burdened with a*[4]
family, had no salary except two hundred florins; and
that want, father of misdeeds, had induced him to
transgress[5]. What does the great Monarch? he commands that the *notes of the trial should be torn up*[6],

replaces him in *his former post* [*the post of before*],
and brings the stipend up to five hundred florins,
saying: "One cannot see all. If such had been always
his *guerdon*⁷ he would not have been unfaithful."

¹impiegato. ²cassa. ³conobbe. ⁴carico di. ⁵prevaricare.
⁶ venga stracciato il processo. ⁷mercede.

²Literally *chest*. ³Seppe is more usual; and as a rule sapere
is to be preferred for mental knowledge, conoscere for knowledge
conveyed by the senses. ⁷More usually rendered *reward*.

54. PAPINIANUS AND JULIUS GRECINUS.

The emperor Caracalla killed his brother Geta in
the very arms of their mother. This man more barbarous than the wild beasts, nevertheless had a horror
to appear a fratricide, and to *gild*¹ in some *sort*² the
atrocious misdeed, he commanded Papinianus, a celebrated *lawyer*³, to compose in his defence a harangue
and to recite it to the senate. "Know," answered
Papinianus, "that it is not for me so easy *to excuse* a
fratricide, as for you it was *to commit* it. Besides,
you would stain yourself with a second crime by
accusing an innocent man after having taken from him
his life. My conscience, my honour *recoil*⁴ from se-
conding you." He had to do with a monster; these
words cost him his life, and Papinianus *fell a victim
to* [*remained victim of*] his integrity.

The same happened to the senator Julius Grecinus,
when Caligula wanted to constrain him to calumniate
Marcus Silvanus, become the object of his hatred.

Grecinus refused at every cost to accuse the innocent, and *as the reward*[5] of so much justice the wretch *caused him to be put* to death.

[1]inorpellare. [2]guisa. [3]giurisconsulto. [4]ripugnano. [5]in premio.

[1]Orpello = tinsel. [3]In the noble style; the common words are legale = lawyer; procuratore = attorney; notaro = notary; avvocato = barrister.

55. Claudius II.

The emperor Claudius II had *had restored* to every one those goods which the unjust Galienus, his predecessor, had *wrested*[1] from them. A poor woman, having heard this, repaired to his presence and said to him: "Know that an officer, by name Claudius, has received *as a* gift from the emperor Galienus an estate which was the only property that I possessed; be it your care *to have it restored to me*." The Sovereign *perceived at once* [*knew quickly*][2] that she intended to speak of him: "*Your request will be granted,*[3]" he answered: "it is *but* [*too*] just that Claudius the emperor should restore that which Claudius the private individual might have of yours."

[1]rapito. [2]conobbe tosto. [3]sarete esaudita.

[2]Conobbe, because such perception is mental sight; he did not know it by learning, or by being told. [3]No literal rendering is possible here, because in English the *person* is *heard*, and the *request* is *granted*.

56. The Beggar made a Mandarin.

Chang-hi a Chinese emperor, being at the chase far from *those who* followed him, encountered an old man who was bitterly weeping, and asked him the *cause* [*motive*] of his tears. "Sir," answered him this unhappy man without knowing him, "I had but one son, my only consolation, my sole hope: a Tartar mandarin has torn him from me and keeps him a slave in his house: behold me therefore deprived of every help. A powerless man, such as I am, how could he obtain justice?" — "This is not *after all*[1] so difficult," answered the Emperor: "That mandarin, of whom you speak to me, *how far hence does he live* [*how much dwells he far from here*]?" — "Two hours *journey* [*of road*], O sir." — "Well; mount *behind*[2] me and guide me to his house." —

The old man obeyed, and meanwhile the guards and the courtiers discovered the road taken by their master, and arrived in time to be witnesses of *an act of justice* [*a justice*] truly *worthy of* a despot of China. The mandarin is convicted of violence, condemned to lose his head, and the sentence *is* executed on the *spot* [*fact*]. The Emperor then addresses to the old man these words: "I assign to thee the post of the dead: profit by his fault to govern according to justice. If thy *faculties* [*lights*] suffice not for this, fail not to advertise me, in order that I may be able to provide for it; and if *conscious of thine own ability* [*recognising thyself clever*], thou renderest thyself unworthy of thy charge, expect for thyself the very fate of him whom I have punished."

[1] poi. [2] in groppa dietro di.

57. Justice preferred[1] to Life.

Some days before the siege of Philipsburg, a grenadier of the army of the Duke of Berwick, having been surprised whilst he was plundering, was condemned to the gallows. As he was a brave soldier, so the officers of his regiment took a lively interest for him, and repaired in a body *to the marshal's tent*[2] to implore his clemency; but in vain. The criminal was led to execution; in the act however that the executioner was about to bind his hands, he found the way to flee and to hide himself in a remote corner of the camp.

The marshal, informed of this flight, commanded that the *military judge* [*auditor*] should suffer the penalty of the grenadier, for not having *watched*[3] sufficiently over the execution of the sentence. This new *convict* [*condemned*] threw himself at the feet of the Duke, protested his own innocence, represented to him the dishonour which thence would redound to his *respectable* [*honest*] family: but reasons, entreaties, tears were thrown to the wind, and the unhappy man must *succumb*[4] to death.

When the grenadier heard the misfortune of the judge, he *emerged*[5] from his *hidingplace*[6], ran to the Duke and said to him: "My General, I am the criminal who has fled: an innocent man is about to die for my cause, he is not the accomplice of my flight; command that he be replaced at once in liberty; death belongs to me; behold me here: I die content." — This action disarmed the marshal, who *pardoned* both.

[1] anteposta. [2] dal maresciallo. [3] invigilato. [4] soggiacere. [5] sbucò. [6] nascondiglio.

² Dal = alla tenda del, because at a siege he would be living
in a tent; otherwise dal = a casa del. Note the 4 equivalents to
the Fr. *chez*. I. With a verb of motion to another's house, da:
"vado da Luigi = je vais chez Louis." II. With a verb of motion
to the house of the subject of the verb, a casa, which includes the
pronoun: "torno a casa = je retourne chez moi; — corse a casa
= il courut chez lui." III. With a verb of station, in casa di: "ella
è restata tre mesi in casa mia, in casa del fratello = elle a passé
trois mois chez moi, chez son frère." IV. In reference to a nation,
fra or presso: "fra gl' Italiani gli amici s'abbracciano, presso
gl' Inglesi si stringon la mano = chez les Italiens les amis s'em-
brassent, chez les Anglais ils se donnent la main." ⁴ Soggiacere
= sotto-giacere = to lie down under = to succumb. There is
also soccombere. ⁵ Buco = hole; sbucare = to issue from a hole.

58. Ottoman Justice.

The lord of Belle-rive, returning from Bender to
Constantinople, met on the road an *Aga*¹ with his
little squadron, who stopped him and asked how much
he had paid of *hire*² for his horses. The foreigner
answered [satisfied] his enquiry. "Thou hast paid *for
them*³ too much," answered the Turk; and this said,
caused to be conducted to his presence the *caravansar*⁴
who was a Greek. "Why hast thou *made this Frank
pay [made pay to this Frank]*," he said to him, "a hire
more *dear [strong]* than [to] others?" — "Sir," answered the Greek, "we *made this agreement [are remained of accord thus]* without *any words arising [that
should be born words]* between us." — "If thy law,"
returned the Aga, "permits thee to exact beyond that
which is due to thee, mine commands me to *cause*
that thou restore this that thou hast received more.

Is it perhaps just that thou overcharge him because he is not of the country? *I have a great mind to order thee to receive a bastinado of a hundred blows* [*There would want little that I should make give to thee a hundred bastinadoes*] on the soles of the feet. *Come*, return to him at once a sequin." — The caravansar *did not let himself be told twice* [*not made repeat to himself the command*]. Oh how *well*[5] would one of these Agas *suit*[5] for every post!

[1] agà.   [2] nolo.   [3] gli.   [4] The same.   [5] To suit well = star bene.

[3] Note that pagare governs the thing paid for in the accusative.

---

59. THE MOST UPRIGHT[1] GENERAL.

The deputies of a city of Germany presented themselves to the Marshal Viscount of Turenne with the offer of a hundred thousand crowns, *if* he would condescend not to make his army pass through their territory. It would not have been difficult to find a person who would have thought to oblige them exceedingly by accepting the offer, promising to content them; but Turenne was a true *gentleman*[2]. "Sirs," he answered, "if the interest of my Prince constrained me to take this road, your gold could not *tempt* [*seduce*] me. Know however, that I should be a thief if I accepted it, because it is not my intention to make the army march *the way you are afraid of* [*by where you fear*]: carry back your money and *set your minds at rest* [*live tranquil*]."

¹integro. ²galantuomo.

¹Give the Eng. noun from this root. What are *integers* in arithmetic? Trace the connexion.

---

60. THE QUAKER WITHOUT IMITATORS.

In the seven years' war, a captain of Austrian ca-
valry had the order to go in quest of forage. He departed at the head of his company, and directed himself to the spot that had been indicated to him. Not
finding it *suitable*¹ to his *purpose* [*intent*], he knocked
at the door of a poor cottage, whereby to find a person
who might point out to him a suitable place. *The
door is opened by* [*Opened the door*] a species of old
Quaker, of whom there are *many* [*several*] also scattered
through Germany. „Good man," said the officer, "*point
out*³ to me a field where I can gather forage for my
horses." — "Very willingly," answered the hermit:
and this said, he *began* at once to precede the company, *advancing-far*⁴ into a valley. They had *gone*
[*made*] a quarter of an hour of *the way* [*road*], when
there presents itself *to their view*⁵ a very fine field of
barley: "Here is exactly that which I need," said the
captain. "Let us *go two steps farther* [*make still two
steps*]," resumed his guide, "and you will *be* [*remain*]
satisfied." — Half a mile farther on they arrive at
another field of barley, and there the old man invites
the soldiers to dismount. They set foot on the ground,
reap the grain, load it on their saddles and remount.
The captain meanwhile says, a little dissatisfied, to the
guide: "But you have made us *go a length* [*do a*

tract] of road *to very little purpose*[6]; the first field
was better than this." — "Yes, sir," answers the old
man; "but that field was not mine."

[1] opportuno. [2] additasse. [3] accennate. [4] innoltrandosi. [5] loro
allo sguardo. [6] molto male a proposito.

[2], [3] Additare from dito; accennare from cenno. [6] Is the English
literal? Would a French rendering be so?

---

61. The Prince more liberal than his Almoner.

The Abbot Quesnel, almoner of the Duke of Pen-
thièvre, had *appointed* [*instituted*]. His Highness *his*
[*for*] universal heir. This virtuous Prince heard that
some *near*[1] relations of the testator were *in poor circumstances* [*ill treated by fortune*], and soon *let* [*made*]
them know, by letter, that the abbot *had made* [*was
fallen into*] a *mistake*[2], *since* [*whilst*] instead of naming
him testamentary executor, as certainly must have been
his intention, he had declared him testamentary heir;
that he certainly could not permit that a *mistake*[2] of
words should bring an *injury*[3] to their rights, and that
he charged himself only with fulfilling in their favour
the commission that by the deceased had been entrusted
to him. *No less was in question than*[4] thirty thousand
francs of revenue, a rich abbey and several other
benefices. This abbot *ill knew his business* [*knew little
his trade*]; the Prince understood it much better
than he.

[1] stretti. [2] equivoco, sbaglio. [3] offesa. [4] non si trattava meno
che di.

²Sbaglio is more general in its meaning; equivoco (as Fr. *équivoque*) implies a mistake as to *words*. Either term can be used here. — "S'è preso equivoco = he has misunderstood."

62. THE JUDGE MAKING RESTITUTION [RESTORER].

M. Gayot de la Réjusse member of the Court of Justice, in the time of a very long audience, tired by the excessive application of the preceding night, had the *mishap* ¹ to let himself *be overcome* ² by sleep, nor woke he *till just as* [*but at the moment in which*] the opinions were being asked. The sentiments were divided, and the victorious *side* ³ was indebted for its advantage only to the superiority of one single vote.

This circumstance excited in the heart of the judge the most lively uneasiness. He feared that his sleep *might possibly have* ⁴ ruined the losing side, nor was there calm for him until he could, in the silence of his closet, examine with the *closest* [*finest*] attention the *documents* [*processes*] of both the parties.

This examination gave him clearly to know how his fears were even too well founded. He doubted not that the cause had been ill *adjudicated* ⁵. In this state of things what does he? He *sends for* [*calls*] the party who had lost, and with his own money reimburses him *both* ⁶ the *capital* ⁷, *and* ⁶ the costs to which he had been condemned.

¹disavventura. ²sopraffare. ³parte. ⁴avesse potuto. ⁵giudicata. ⁶tanto — quanto. ⁷capitale.

³Parte = party in a law-suit; always feminine, as you must remember in writing this exercise. ⁷Masc. in this sense; fem. when it means *capital city*, because città is understood.

63. WHERE VIRTUE MAY GO TO BURROW[1].

The celebrated Molière and the musician Charpentier were *on their way* [*directed*] from Auteuil to Paris. A poor man *having presented himself at the door*[2] of their carriage, the poet *gave* [*made*] him alms, and the carriage departed. A moment after they heard the mendicant who pursuing them *with all his might* [*breath*][3], was crying, "Stop, stop!" The coachman suspends his course, and the *beggar*[4] draws near *once more* [*another time*] to his benefactor and says to him: "Sir, *you have made a mistake*[5]: you had certainly not the intention to give me a louis; behold I return it to you." — "Where ever has virtue burrowed!" exclaims Molière; "hold, worthy man, here is another for thee."

[1] si vada a cacciar. [2] essendosi affacciato all' adito. [3] a tutta lena. [4] pitocco. [5] vi siete ingannato.

[1] Cacciar cannot be the last word, no elision is made at the end of a sentence; this suggests the construction. [2] adito = entrance, passage, way. [5] Ingannare, ingannarsi = Fr. *tromper*, *se tromper*.

---

64. A GENTLEMAN[1] WITHOUT POSTERITY[2].

The poet Scarron, by dint of making others laugh, reduced himself to have to *bewail*[3] himself, necessitated to sell his own goods to be able to pay his debts. Among those who presented themselves to *buy them* [*make the acquisition of them*] there was a certain M. Nublé, who bought some for the sum of eighteen thousand livres, reposing blindly, *in regard*[4] to the price, on the noted probity of the vendor.

The affair being-consummated *to the* [*with*] satisfaction of both the parties, the buyer passed to a minute examination of this his new property, to do with it that which was most suitable, and he perceived that he had bought it at too *mean*[5] a price. In consequence of this discovery *he went*[6] to visit M. Scarron, who had made a sale *like a* true poet, and said to him: "Your estates, *according*[7] to an exact estimate which *I had made*, are not worth *indeed* eighteen thousand, but twentyeight thousand livres: *be pleased therefore that I should make up for*[8] that which still I owe you;" — and on the *spot*[9] counted out to him the *overplus*[10]. — Where are gone these M. Nublé?

[1]galantuomo. [2]discendenza. [3]compiangere. [4]rapporto. [5]meschino. [6]portossi. [7]a tenore. [8]gradite perciò ch io supplisca a. [9]fatto stesso. [10]soprappiù.

---

65. Probity preferred to Love.

At Bologna, a *person of quality* [*qualified person*][1] who had *begun living on an expensive scale* [*placed himself on a footing very costly*][2] not being able longer *to keep it up*[3], saw himself constrained to retire with his family into one of his estates. There dwelt not far from him an old merchant who had an only daughter, generally esteemed, not only for the *abundance of his possessions*,[4] but also for his eminent qualities; who *as soon as he considered himself to have realized a sufficient fortune* [*since he knew sufficiently secured his fortune*], had resolved to *give up trade* [*renounce every commerce*].

The proximity of their habitation *caused*[5] that they *contracted a* [*bound together*] close friendship: they saw each other every day and treated each other with much familiarity. The *gentleman*[6] reflecting on the disorder of his domestic finances and on the impossibility of leaving to a son, who deserved *on every account* [*by every title*] his tenderness, a fortune capable of sustaining the lustre of his name, he thought that that of the merchant *would be* most-adapted to repair his; and in order to effect this project, he determined to ask of his friend the hand of his daughter, for his son. And so much the more he felt himself inclined to embrace this course, as his desire *made evident to him* [*made transpire to him*] between those two young people the first sparks of a reciprocal inclination.

The *upright*[7] merchant, grateful for the honour that was offered him, and to which he would not have dared to aspire, *thought it nevertheless his*[8] duty before consenting to it, to place under the eye of that personage the disproportion of this *connexion* [*knot*] with respect to birth; but the personal qualities of the *girl*[9], the *excellent* [*beautiful*] education by her received, a beginning of reciprocal inclination which at least was *guessed at* [*interpreted*], served to smooth every difficulty.

The father delayed not to communicate to the son the project, and the assent which he had received from the father of the *girl*[9]. This news surprised the son, who although he esteemed the young woman and felt his heart much disposed to love her, yet expected not to find himself pushed *unexpectedly*[10] to *conclude* [*en-counter*] this sort of precipitate marriage. He *failed*[11] not therefore to *make evident*[12] a certain air of cold irresolution, and to adduce some not contemptible difficulties. "My son," said to him then the gentleman, "I am at last constrained, *to* [*with*] my extreme regret, to *tear*[13] the bandage from thine eyes. We have not retired *without cause* [*for nothing*] into this castle. Thou perhaps thinkest to be still a very rich person; but observe, my dear, this *balance-sheet*[14], which presents the true state of the family: reflect on the debts, on the credits, on the possessions; subject it *by all means*[15] to minute examination; I leave it *therefore*[16] in thy hands, and judge by this *truthful*[17] paper how reasonable is my proposition. Tomorrow I await answer."

The son *withdrew*[18]; and having - examined *the state of his affairs* [*his economical state*], *learned* only too well *to* his grief that the sum of the debts absorbed *nearly all the property*[19]. He passed the night *racked*[20] by bitterness, and yet more by the sight of the sacrifice which probity *commanded*[21] him to make of a passion so much more dear to his heart as it was more pure and *fresh* [*nascent*]. He rises the day following *early*[22], while his father still slept, and repairs to the house of the merchant. He *causes to be announced* to him his *eagerness*[23] to communicate to him a thing of high *import*[24], and *is* soon introduced into his bed-chamber. There, triumphing, gentleman as he was *considered to be* [*held*], *over the shrinking from*[25] revealing to him his secret poverty, and over the *grief*[26] of being obliged to speak of it against the *inclinations* [*tendencies*] of his heart, ingenuously he said to him: "Yesterday my father had the goodness

9

to ask of you for me your daughter in *marriage*
[*wife*]²⁷; but I *feel*²⁸ not *courage* [*heart*], O sir, to
deceive [*make fall into deception*] you and that good
girl. You are upright enough for *me to be*²⁹ certain
that the delicate *secret I confide to you* [*confidence
which I make you*] in this moment, will remain covered
by the most religious silence. Behold in this paper,
which I received from *my father's own hands*, the
unfortunate [*sinister*] state in which our family actually
finds itself. Be on guard over your fate and over that
of your daughter."

"Ah! sir," answered the merchant, with tears in
his eyes, "I held you, *truth to tell*³⁰, as very rich
person; but it was not *known*³¹ to me that *you had
attained such a height of* [*to so much really reached
your*] virtue. If my daughter is not to you *unpleasing*³²,
if you *deem her worthy* [*deign her*] of so much, I hope
that *you having* her *as your* [*in*] wife, my fortune will
be able to compensate you for that which has failed you,
nor doubt I that managed [*directed*] by a young man
of so much merit, it can be sufficient to our common
happiness."

A marriage that *started*³³ from such principles had
the most fortunate *success* [*issue*]³⁴. *On this event might
be based an interesting play* [*Behold an event which,
enriched by the imagination, would be dear to the
scene*].

²dispendioso. ³sostenerlo. ⁴copia degli averi. ⁵fece sì.
⁶signore. ⁷probo. ⁸si credette nondimeno in. ⁹fanciulla, ragazza.
¹⁰impensatamente. ¹¹lasciò. ¹²palesare. ¹³strappare. ¹⁴bilancio.
¹⁵pure. ¹⁶perciò. ¹⁷veridica. ¹⁸appartossi. ¹⁹pressochè tutte
le facoltà. ²⁰straziato. ²¹imponeva. ²²di buon mattino. ²³premura. ²⁴rilievo. ²⁵del ribrezzo di. ²⁶angustia. ²⁷isposa. ²⁸mi

sento. ²⁹essere io. ³⁰a vero dire. ³¹poi noto. ³²discara. ³³par-
tiva. ³⁴esito.

¹Always fem. as in Fr. ⁴, ⁷Give Eng. words from the same
roots. ⁶Why not galantuomo, as so often lately? Because signore,
like gentiluomo, designates a gentleman by birth; galantuomo, if
used for gentleman, one who is so by his moral qualities. ⁹Fanciulla denotes, not any particular age, but the state of being unmarried; whereas fanciullo, ragazzo, ragazza, are used of children
and young unmarried persons only. ¹²From what adj. is this verb
formed? ¹³Strappare = to tear = wrench from. Stracciare, la-
cerare = to tear in pieces. ¹⁴But bilancia = scales, balance.
¹⁶Perciò may refer alike to what precedes or follows; pertanto
only to what precedes. ¹⁷Veridica = che dice il vero. ¹⁸Appartossi = se n ando a parte = he went *apart*. ¹⁹Facoltà = property,
is plural. ²⁴Rilievo is primarily *relief*, i. e. rising out of a plane
surface. So we use *salient* for *striking*. ²⁵Ribrezzo, primarily
shivering-fit; hence any physical or moral shrinking. ²⁶From
angusto, narrow; what *contracts* the heart, whereas joy enlarges it.
— "Mi si stringe il cuore = my heart contracts;" in idiomatic
English, "sinks." ²⁷Sposa is usually better. But wherever a word
has two forms, the one beginning with s impura, the other with i,
the latter is preferred after a preposition ending in a consonant.
Why? ²⁸Note the idiomatic refl. pron. ³¹Note the untranslatable
idiomatic expletive. ³²Literally —?

---

66. The Vinedresser ¹ who will not buy cheap.

Claude Pechon, of the village of Mombré-les-Reims,
at the age of fiftyeight years, a poor vinedresser, father
of eight children, received into his house a sick brother-
in-law of his, in virtue of a contract, by which Claude
obliged himself to maintain him *during his life*², and
the other ceded to him the property of a field, *valued*³
four hundred livres.

9 *

Two days after the consummation of this contract, the invalid died. Claude, against the advice of the parish-priest and of the notary, replaced in possession of the field the heirs of the dead, saying that he would not *gain* [*acquire*], *to* [*with*] their damage, four hundred livres so cheap.

[1] vignaio.　[2] sua vita durante.　[3] valutato.

[2] A legal form of expression.

---

67. THE ALMS-GIVING POOR-WOMAN[1], AND THE POOR-MAN WHO WILL NOT BE SO.

In the past century, in several places of Saxony had been introduced the custom of making, *from time to time* [*from when to when*][2] some general *collections*[3] *in* [*to*] relief of the poor, and the *elders*[4] of the parish were *at once* [*together*] collectors and distributors of it. It happened that those of one village entered into the house of an old woman, in order to insert her name in the catalogue of the poor-women who had a right to the public beneficence. She was occupied *in unwinding*[5] her thread from the *reel*[6], in a dark little room, whose furniture attested very eloquently the misery of the mistress.

The little-old-woman, informed of the object of this visit, went out of the room without speaking, and returned to it a moment after with a coin in her hand. "*Take* [*Hold*] here a *groschen*[7]," she said, "which I have *borrowed*[8], and which I will restore immediately that I shall have finished my *skeins*[9]. There are per-

sons more poor than I; *give* [*make*] them this alms:
my name must not be written in that list, so long as
I have so much of strength *as*[10] to be able to raise
the water from the well: God guard me from it! I
should think *I was stealing* [*to steal*] from some-one
who is more helpless than I; *go, and God be with you*
[*go with God*]."

Joseph Heloir, a shoemaker of Paris, was of the
same sentiment. In age more than octogenarian, he
hears that some charitable persons *are exerting themselves* [*give themselves anxiety*][11] in order to procure
for him an alms from the Philanthropic Society, and
sends them word [*causes them to be warned*] that they
must prefer *those who are poorer than he* [*the more
poor*] to him, because, praise to Heaven, he enjoys a
pension of a hundred and fifty livres, and the *leavings*[12]
of the table of a neighbouring house.

[1] pitocca elemosiniera. [2] di quando in quando. [3] collette.
[4] anziani. [5] a svolgere. [6] naspo. [7] grosso. [8] preso ad imprestito.
[9] gomitoli. [10] da. [11] premura. [12] avanzi.

[2] Remember this pretty and frequent idiom, and note the prepositions; they are the same in the literal rendering di tempo in
tempo. [3] Colletta, a *collection* of money; also a *collect*. [4] From
the same root as *ancient*. [6] Hence innaspare = to wind. [8] Literally
taken on loan.

---

68. THE HONOURABLE[1] PORTER, AND THE WOMAN WHO
PRAYS [MAKES PRAYER][2] AGAINST HER OWN INTEREST.

At the fair of Beaucaire, a porter of Gange found
by chance a most beautiful *repeater* [*watch with*[3] *repe-*

tition], and, having-repaired at once to the public crier[4], charged him to *cry it* [*make the publications of it*] on all the *street-corners*[5] near to the spot where he had found it; and because *for this purpose* [*to this effect*] *were wanted*[6] thirty pence, and he had not but eight, he borrowed the twenty-two that *were lacking*[7]. The owner appeared, and the worthy man delayed not a moment to restore to him the watch.

But better still than he, a poor widow, burdened with four little children, showed herself solicitous to seek out the master of a little bag of money, found by her on the public road which from Strasburg leads to Savernes. Having-made all possible *researches* [*examinations*], finally *she succeeded in learning* [*it succeeded to her to know*] that that money belonged to a lady who had *stayed*[8] in an inn not far from the place where she had lost the bag. She brought it immediately to its owner, refusing every recompense, on the *ground*[9] that she had done *after all*[10] only her duty. In the act however of leaving, *remembering* [*reflecting*] to have *incurred* [*encountered*] an expense for this affair, she *stops* [*suspends the step*], and says *turning* [*turned*] to the lady: "*If you do not object* [*it displeases you not*], Madam, deign to *give*[11] me three livres which I gave to the Conventual Fathers for the celebration of two Masses, to the end that I might be able to find the owner of the bag." — What probity!

---

[1] onorato. [2] orazione. [3] a. [4] banditore. [5] capi-strada. [6] occorreano. [7] mancavano. [8] trattenuta. [9] fondamento. [10] alfine. [11] donare.

[1] Onorato may mean *honourable* as well as *honoured*. [2] Fare orazione = pregare; but the latter term might be used of requesting a fellow-creature. [3] Note that when, as here, no article is

required, the prep. *a* is used, as in Fr., to introduce a descriptive circumstance; — *moulin à vent* = mulino a vento. But when the article is required, the Ital. prep. is da; — *l'homme au manteau noir* = l'uomo dal mantello nero. [4]From bandire = to proclaim. [6]Occorrere = to be needful. — "Mi occorrono due lire sterline = I am in want of £2." — But compare the construction. [9]Like our expression "my opinion is *founded* on these reasons." [11]As was formerly explained, this verb, formed from dono, is used only of *making a present;* and therefore shews more remarkable delicacy and disinterestedness in the speaker than dare would have done.

---

69. THE CAPTAIN WHO VOLUNTARILY DEGRADES HIMSELF.

A young-man about to take a wife, called instead to *draw* [*extract*] from the urn the billet, by which he was in danger of *being obliged to*[1] undertake the military career, thought to serve better his ends if for one year *he should enrol himself as*[2] volunteer. To this effect he repaired to M. de Mitry, captain in the regiment of the guards of Lorraine, and begged him to receive him on such condition into his company. The officer consented to it.

Completed the year, the soldier recalled to his superior the made promise, and the latter *suggested* [*insinuated*] to him to present himself to the colonel of the regiment and to beg him to *sign* [*subscribe*] his *discharge*[3]. The youth made the request: but was not heard, under pretext that he was a brave soldier and that he *was very well suited* [*suited much*] to his corps.

This repulse pierced the heart of the lover who was from day to day awaited by his bride, and already *he turned over in his*[4] mind to desert. But his captain

remained not less afflicted than he, and willed at every
cost to *redeem his pledge* [*disengage the given faith*].
He awaited a day on which the officers of the regiment
were gathered together, and having repaired to the
meeting, with the young-man at his side, presented
himself to the colonel and said to him, "Behold a soldier to whom I promised his discharge; and since a
man of honour must not be wanting to his word, and
you, *besides*[5], will not *set him at* [*replace him in*]
liberty in order not to lose a good soldier, so I renounce even from this moment the grade of captain,
and will carry, in his stead, the *knapsack*[6]." Such
unexpected proposal, which in itself was not acceptable,
constrained at last the colonel to *give way* [*surrender
himself*].

[1] dover.　[2] si fosse arrolato qual.　[3] congedo.　[4] ravvolgea in.
[5] d'altronde.　[6] giberna.

[3] The former note on licenza applies also to congedo.

70.　THE FATHER WHO SAVES THE SLAYER OF HIS SON.

Not [*Little*] far from Seville, a Spanish cavalier
fought against a Moorish gentleman and killed him.
Some officers of justice who saw at some distance the
duel, set themselves to pursue the slayer to arrest him,
as the law imposed; but the latter, fleeing, *met*[1]
without their *perceiving*, *with the*[2] wall of a garden,
climbed up it[3] and descended in a *path*[4], along which
was walking the owner. At the first seeing him, he
threw himself at his feet, manifested to him his danger,

implored his *protection*[5], and conjured him to will to
deliver [*withdraw*] him from the rigour of justice.

The gentleman, being-moved by his situation, took
him by hand, and *hastily* [*hasty*] conducted him to a
closet, situated at the bottom of the same garden, promising him that being-arrived the night, he would
favour [*would have favoured*] his escape.

Pass few instants, and behold *there is brought* [*to
be conducted*] to the palace of that gentleman the
corpse of his *dead* [*extinct*] son. What *horror*[6]! what
dismay[7]! The indications that *are* given to him permit
him not to doubt that *the very* [*precisely the*] Spaniard,
to whom he has promised safety, is the homicide.
The most unhappy father retires into his room, refuses
to see any one [*to will to see whomever*], and abandons
himself, until night, in prey to two opposite affections,
to the grief of having lost a son and to the impulse
to avenge his death. But that which presents itself at
last more vividly to the *mind* [*spirit*], is the given
word to save the homicide, and' this sentiment of honour triumphs in that great soul over all the others.
He descends intrepid therefore into the garden, opens
with his own hand the door of the closet, commands
the Spaniard to follow him, guides him to the *stable*[8],
makes him mount on one of his best *steeds*[9] and says
to him: "The young-man whom thou killedst is my
son; but I have given thee word to save thee: *go*[10];
I leave to God the care to avenge me."

---

[1] si avvenne. [2] avvedimento, nel. [3] vi si arrampicò. [4] viale.
[5] patrocinio. [6] raccapriccio. [7] sbigottimento. [8] scuderia. [9] destrieri.
[10] vattene.

³Arrampicarsi is from the same root as our *rampant*. ⁶Racca-pricciare = to stand on end. — "His hair stood on end with horror = raccapricciò". ⁸The Fr. *écurie*: — from scudo, shield. ⁹A noble term. ¹⁰The Fr. va t'en.

---

71. VIRTUE HAS TRIUMPHED OVER [1] SEX.

Groaning under a tyrannical yoke the Athenians, they determined to shake it off and to liberate their country from the oppressor. In the number of the conspirators there was also a woman, by name Leæna, of which was informed the tyrant when he came to discover the first threads of this plot. *He trusting to obtain his end through her* [*Confiding he in the*] *womanly* [2] weakness, she was amongst the first arrested, nor was there any kind of torments to which the cruel one did not subject her whereby to wring from her mouth the name of the accomplices and the web of the conspiracy. She sustained the *trial* [3] with the most heroic constancy: but since with her strength she felt fail her courage, assailed by the *dread* [*uneasiness*] of being able to betray, in the excess of her pains, the secret, she came to the *cruel* [4] resolution to lop with her teeth her tongue, to render herself impotent to speak. When *the Athenians succeeded* [5] in shaking off the yoke, it was their first *care* [*attention*] to erect to this heroine a statue, representing her under the form of a lioness, and on the pedestal that supported it they placed the inscription: *Virtue has triumphed over sex.* See how the secret *kept* [6] by woman *received, up* [7] to those days, the celebrity *of a* [8] prodigy!

¹, ⁸del. ²muliebre. ³cimento. ⁴cruda. ⁵agli Ateniesi riuscì. ⁶custodito. ⁷riscuotesse, sino.

³More literally *conflict.* ⁴Sometimes better rendered *harsh, hard.* ⁸Celebrity belongs to a prodigy *as such,* and *always;* therefore *prodigio* is here a common noun used in a general sense, and takes the def. art.

72. Artifice to oblige a Thief to restitution.

Alphonso king of Arragon, accompanied by several courtiers, entered into shop of a jeweller, *desirous*¹ to examine a collection of diamonds. *Scarcely had the King gone out when*² the merchant overtook him and *softly*³ made him *aware* [*participator*] that *he had* [*to him was*] in that moment *missed*⁴ a jewel of the highest value. Some reasons moved the King to be not *altogether*⁵ easy about the probity of one of the *retinue*⁶; but that was not the circumstance to act *according to the*⁷ tenor of his suspicions: *one had to*⁸ keep secret the thief, if indeed there was one, and oblige him nevertheless to restitution. He resolved therefore to return into the shop with all his suite, and *having entered* [*entered that he was*], he commanded the merchant to place in the midst a great vase full of *bran*⁹. He ordered then all the bystanders to bury in it, the one after the other, the closed hand and to withdraw it thence open. The ceremony being finished, the bran was overturned upon a table and the diamond was found.

¹bramoso. ²uscitone appena il re. ³sommessamente. ⁴mancata. ⁵affatto. ⁶comitiva. ⁷a. ⁸doveasi. ⁹crusca.

73. The Female who knows to keep silence.

One night, at Venice, in *the depth of winter*[1], the *parish priest*[2] of St. Moses, a man more than septuagenarian, was about *to go to bed*[3]; when the woman who served him, in the act of *putting down*[4] on the ground the warmingpan, saw underneath a pair of legs of man in ambush to *seize*[5] the opportune moment to commit some crime. Who would not, at this discovery, have *uttered*[6] a cry? And yet the woman, against the disposition of her sex, capable of bridling the tongue, gave not the least indication of what she had seen; she took the light, and *having-wished*[7] good night to her master, shut him into the chamber.

Having-done this, she descended the staircase, and having-drawn the *cord*[8] of a bell that passed through a room, she feigned that in the street one rang to desperation. She opened the window, and, having-simulated a rapid dialogue, ran with the light anew to the door of her master, opened it and warned him that he must hastily dress himself, because there was in peril of death a person, of whom she told the name, who implored his assistance.

The parish priest, *waited on by the maid*[9], re-dressed himself, and both went out of the chamber, into which she, *having-turned*[10] the key, shut the culprit.

It was then that she revealed to her master the *secret*[11]. They sent at once for the civic guard, who seized the delinquent in the fact. — The Athenians would have *immortalized*[12] with a statue the *masculine and ready-witted*[13] silence of this woman.

¹di fitto verno. ²parroco. ³coricarsi. ⁴deporre. ⁵cogliere.
⁶gettato. ⁷augurata. ⁸filo. ⁹servito dalla fantesca. ¹⁰girata.
¹¹arcano. ¹²eternato. ¹³maschile ed arguto.

¹Fitto is from figgere, to infix. Used with regard to the
seasons, it means *the height* of summer, *the depth* of winter.
³Fr. *se coucher*. ⁶Fr. *pousser un cri*. Indeed the Eng. *utter*
(a form of *outer*) is properly = to throw *out*, give *outward*
expression to. ⁹Fantesca, fem. of fante.

---

74. TOTILA KING OF THE GOTHS.

Who knows not the humane and generous action
of the great Henry, who blockading straitly Paris,
having heard what a multitude of peaceable citizens
found themselves exposed to cruel famine, commanded
that victuals should be by stealth introduced into the
place, *although it was his enemy* [*although enemy*]?
But not *equally well*¹ known is the trait of singular
humanity used by Totila, when he constrained Naples,
by him besieged, to surrender itself at last through
famine. He foresaw that, *opened wide*² the gates, the
*famished*³ vanquished would have *eagerly thrown*⁴
themselves on the provisions already prepared, and that
the *greediness*⁵, by loading of too much the stomach
*exhausted*⁶ of strength, would have cost to many their
life. He *had* them therefore *shut* again, and *had introduced* into the city successive portions of *food easy
of digestion* [*easy food*], defended by guards, the which
food *was to be* distributed to each with *frugal*⁷ hand,
then gradually increased in the quality and in the dose:
whence it *happened* [*came*] that, the *powers*⁸ being-
restored without danger, the greater number acknow-

ledged their life *to be owing to* [*from*] this paternal attention of the victor.

¹del pari. ²spalancate. ³famelici. ⁴avidamente lanciati. ⁵ingordigia. ⁶sfinito. ⁷parca. ⁸forze.

²From palanca, a pale. ³From fame.

---

75. THE HEROIC PHILANTHROPY.

The *ground floor*¹ of a house of the city of Auch was in prey to the flames, *when*² the people ran to extinguish the conflagration, accompanied by their bishop, Mgʳ Dampchon, who animated them to the work. When at a window of the first floor *shewed herself suddenly*³ a mother who held in her arms an infant, and who with tears and with cries implored succour: the flames were about to devour her.

*There was put up against the*⁴ wall a ladder, but it was necessary that some one should mount to the *top*⁵, in order to protect the descent of these unhappy-ones. The bishop proposed a recompense to whoever *might have* the courage to reach to them a hand, *but no one* [*nor any one*] presented himself, and the peril grew meanwhile. He offered a prize still greater, nor was for this listened to; he *went so far as* [*arrived even*] to promise an annual pension of a thousand livres, and none dared venture. "I will go then my-self," exclaimed this rare prelate, and *this said*⁶ mounts the ladder which the flame threatens to *catch* [*kindle*]. Arrived at the height of the window, Heaven blesses his efforts; it seems that the fire respects his *merciful*⁷ intention : he descends happily with the two victims snatched from the devouring flames.

And not less worthy of admiration is that which happened at Nancy in the year 1776. — The conflagration was *so much the more fearful in that*[8] a most violent wind increased extremely its activity, and the houses were almost all of wood. *Whirlwinds*[9] of smoke, of *embers*[10], of *lighted soot*[11] were rising to the sky, the angry flames *burst forth on*[12] every side; here and there *fell in*[13] the roofs, *a general downfall was feared to be imminent* [*was feared imminent a general downfall*][14]; nor to anything else *now* [*more*] tended the labours than to impede the *progress* [*progresses*] of the *devastating*[15] fire.

Amid the howls of despair, the groans of avarice, the tumults of rapine, the efforts of beneficence, a woman by the august character of her grief drew to herself the *gaze* [*looks*] of the multitude, and this was a mother who, *in* [*on*] the street, on her knees, with her hands *upturned*[16] to heaven, with her eyes immovablé on the flames, *called help*[17] for two infants, in an instant in which fright had surprised her tenderness abandoned by her in the room of a fourth floor, towards which the flames were advancing boldly.

A danger that affrighted the most intrepid rendered barren the pity *awakened*[18] in each by this miserable woman. But *to her come forward*[19] two grenadiers of the royal regiment who, raising her from the ground, *ask her about*[20] the internal structure of that house. Scarcely has she pronounced a few words, with inconceivable intrepidity *they push forward*[21] between flame and flame, a cloud of smoke snatches them from the eyes of all, and having-passed some moments, a part

of that house *falls headlong*[22]. At the *noise*[23] of the
fall, the terrified mother loses her last hope, and falls
to earth *swooning* [*swooned*].

Leaping from beam to beam that burns, behold
reappear the two grenadiers: they bear lighted here
and there the *skirts*[24] of their clothes, their hair is
already *in ashes, scorched*[25] their face and their hands;
but their soul is all rapt by the sublimity of the action
which they have performed; and the one and the
other has in his arms an infant which they *give again*[26]
to the maternal bosom. The woman *gradually recovers*
[*goes resuming*] the use of her senses and clasps the
pledges of her love, amid the acclamations of the
people astonished or *affected*[27], and the *crash*[28] of the
house which *completely falls in* [*finishes to shake*].[29]

[1] piano terreno. [2] allorchè. [3] si scoprì improvvisamente.
[4] venne appoggiata al. [5] sommità. [6] ciò detto. [7] pietosa. [8] tanto
più spaventevole quanto che. [9] vortici. [10] brage. [11] fuliggine
accesa. [12] sbucavano per. [13] si sprofondavano. [14] crollo. [15] devastatore. [16] rivolte. [17] gridava aiuto. [18] destata. [19] le si affacciano.
[20] la ricercano intorno. [21] s'innoltrano. [22] precipita. [23] fragore.
[24] lembi. [25] inceneriti, abbrustolati. [26] ridonano. [27] intenerito.
[28] scroscio. [29] termina di crollare.

[6] In this expression always ciò, not questo. Ciò is the proper
demonstrative pronoun when the antecedent is a clause. [7] Merciful
is also misericordioso; but this is chiefly used of mercy shewn to
a culprit, and even then *clemente* is often preferred. [15] Note that
you here, use an adj. and one which has the termination of a noun;
not, as you might have expected, a present participle or verbal adjective. [17] An idiomatic form. [18] Svegliare is not used in a figurative sense. [23] A more noble term than rumore, and somewhat
stronger.

76. The noble and compassionate Butcher.

Being-dead at Berlin the merchant Kruger, a man of signal probity and of poor fortunes, he left his widow with four children, masters *indeed*[1] of the house by them inhabited, but necessarily constrained to *offer it for* [*expose it to*] sale to satisfy the rights of the creditors.

George Ernest Teichmann, a butcher by profession, but a person of excellent heart, *contrived* [*went meditating*] a project by which the widow and the little orphans should not be deprived of a habitation. *He took counsel*[2] on this *head* [*article*] with his wife, of a soul as beneficent as his, and they resolved together that, the house being-put to auction, they would be the buyers, to do afterwards to the family Kruger all *the good they possibly could* [*that good which best by them could-be*][3].

The good George succeeded in making the *purchase* [*acquisition*] of it for only four thousand two hundred and twentyfive *crowns*[4], while it was worth much more. Highly pleased with *what he had effected*[5], he repaired to the widow and held to her this discourse: "Madam, I am the buyer of this house, but you must stay in it. You will not have any other *charge*[6] except that of paying me the ordinary *interest* [*profit*] of the sum disbursed, and this also will serve to extinguish the four hundred crowns owed me by your husband. Meanwhile you and I will seek a new buyer who *may purchase* this habitation for that which it is worth really, and all the overplus which *we shall succeed in obtaining*[7], beyond my capital, will be *solely*[8] for you."

10

Thus in fact it happened. An innkeeper *considering
it very suitable for an inn* [*having-found it very opportune to make of it inn*], applied [*turned himself*] to the
butcher to make the *purchase*. "Repair," he answered,
"to the widow Kruger and treat with her: *I have no
claim* [*cannot claim*] [9] on that house except the sum
that I disbursed: all that which you will give her
more, is of her *right* [10] " The contract was concluded
with Mrs. Kruger for six thousand five hundred crowns,
by which she *in fact obtained* [*came to obtain*] a gift,
beyond the remainder, of two thousand two hundred
and seventyfive crowns from the compassionate and
noble soul of a butcher.

[1] bensì. [2] consigliossi. [3] si potesse. [4] scudi. [5] l'operato.
[6] carico. [7] ne verrà fatto di conseguire. [8] unicamente. [9] pretendere.
[10] ragione.

[9] As in French. [10] This word often means *right*.

---

77. The Sultan Saladin.

Beneficence, to speak properly, is every gift that,
in distinction from acts of mere humanity [*to difference
from the humane acts*], is *least* [*less*] *expected* [1] from
him who does it, and *least* sought by him who receives
it. Who would say that a Sultan of Syria and of
Egypt, a *mussulman* [2] prince, warlike and a conqueror,
was, for his rectitude and beneficence, bewailed, when
he died, by the Christians themselves? And yet such
was Saladin, whose sentiments are *a forcible* [3] reproof
to several of us who vaunt ourselves to profess a reli-

gion of love. Arrived at his last illness, in place of
the standard which before *fluttered*[4] over his door, he
caused to be spread[5] the cloth in which was to be
wrapped his corpse, and ordered that *beside it*[6] a herald
should cry: "Behold all that which Saladin, subduer
of the East, carries with him of the *conquests achieved*
[*made conquests*]." He willed *too*[7] by his testament
that there should be lavished most copious alms, but
however distributed in equal portions, as much to the
poor Mussulmans as to the Christians and to the Jews,
leaving written these *golden*[8] words; "All men are
brothers, and when assisting them *is in question*[9], one
must not[10] inform oneself of that which they believe,
but of that which they suffer."

[1] atteso.　　[2] musulmano.　　[3] forte.　　[4] sventolava.　　[5] spiegare.
[6] accanto.　　[7] poi.　　[8] auree.　　[9] si tratta di.　　[10] non bisogna.

[4] From vento.　　[5] Literally *to unfold*. The root?

---

78. Admirable Accord between Doctrine and Practice.

The celebrated Gessner, professor of *moral philosophy* [*morality*] at Leipsic, *applied himself in one of
his lectures* [*made himself in a lesson*] to treat of the
right which the unfortunate have to the general compassion and beneficence; and this man, endowed with
delicate fancy and with exquisite sentiment, knew in
such wise to colour his picture, that he wrung tears
from the eyes of several of his hearers.

One of them, moved to curiosity to know if the
actions of the professor were in harmony with the

preachings, *disguised* [*masked*] himself as a gentleman beggar, and, having-presented himself in the room, simulating an air of sadness and of *shyness*[1], *set forth* [*exposed to him*] his deplorable circumstances and the *pressing* [*strait*] need that he had of sixty livres to pay at once a debt, without which he *would be arrested* [*would have been made prisoner*].

"This is precisely all my substance," answered Gessner; "I am however fortunate if with so scanty a sum I can so much benefit you." He went to fetch this money and consigned it to the suppliant, who thanking him, promised him to restore it *at the end of*[2] one month. "Do not incommode yourself, no, my dear," said the professor; "although I be poor" (and he was *so* in fact, as he was *so* always, "nevertheless I will wait *as long as* [*as much as*] shall please you: go; God give you better fate."

The young man then *knelt down*, and kissing his hand *repeatedly*[3], craved of him pardon for the experiment to which he had willed to subject his virtue.

"And how ever," said Gessner, embracing him with transport, "could you doubt of my *inclination*[4] to assist the unhappy? Suppose you me one insensible to pleasure? and is there perhaps in the world a pleasure more vivid than that of doing good to one's fellow. creatures? It is as necessary to my soul as is food to my body; and believe me, my friend, that *if* I could no longer succour the unfortunate, this my want not satisfied would bring me to death."

Give me all the rich with the heart of M. Gessner, and then know how to tell me what the world will become.

149

¹ritrosia. ²in capo ad. ³a più riprese. ⁴propensione.

³Fr. *à plusieurs reprises.*

79. THE BENEFICENT MISER.

The commissioners charged to make a collection in
London, for the hospital of Bedlam, presented themselves at the door of a house that was *ajar* ¹. They
opened it softly, and whilst they found themselves at
the foot of the staircase, they heard the voice of an
old-man *angry* ² with his maidservant, because, after
having [*she*] *used a match* ³ to kindle the fire, she had
stupidly ⁴ thrown away the rest, when she might instead
have replaced it for another occasion.

After *a good laugh* ⁵ between themselves on the
importance of this subject of anger, they, rather through
curiosity to know this original than *because they flattered themselves they should obtain anything [through
flattery of obtaining* ⁶ *something]* mounted the staircase
and presented themselves to the old man, to whom they
exposed the *cause [argument]* of their visit. The latter,
without either welcoming them, or dismissing them,
having-pronounced an "I have heard," turned *his back
on them [to them his shoulders]* ⁷. They stood *awhile* ⁸
to look the one at the other and to smile; but when
they were already on the point of going away, reappeared the *churl* ⁹ and counted to them four hundred
guineas *for [to]* the charitable object.

Struck by such unexpected generosity, *they did
not succeed in fully dissembling* their amazement;
which ¹⁰ he having-perceived, asked them of the motive,

and the commissioners ingenuously confessed to him
that they knew not how to reconcile [*not to know to
accord*] the quantity of the offering with the affair of
the match, heard by them by accident *while* [*in the*]
mounting the staircase. "Sirs," he answered them
abruptly, "I have my mode of saving and my mode
of spending; the one *feeds*[11] the other, and they are
both to my taste. In matter of beneficence, count
always on those who use matches twice." The saying
this and the shutting the door of the room *in* [*on*]
their face was the same thing. Let us pardon inci-
vility to one who makes alms of four hundred guineas
at a time.

[1]socchiusa. [2]incollerito. [3]adoperato un solfanello. [4]balor-
damente. [5]una risata. [6]buscar. [8]alquanto. [9]burbero. [10]del
che. [11]alimenta.

[2]From what noun? [3]Solfanello, from solfo, sulphur. [7]In
this and many other idiomatic and familiar expressions, spalle is
the equivalent to *back*.

80. Xenocrates.

Alexander the Macedonian had in so much consideration Xenocrates, that he sent to him deputies with
the gift of fifty talents, a sum which surpassed the
fifty thousand crowns of our money. *On their arrival*
[*Being-arrived they*] at the house of the philosopher,
he invited them to supper, which was as frugal as they
ought to have expected [*it*] from a professor of the
most austere morality. The day after they interrogated
him where they *were* [*had*] to deposit the talents:

"The supper of yesterday," answered Xenocrates, "ought to have *shewn* [*instructed*] you that I have no need of money. *You will return it*[1] therefore to your master, warning him that he is *bound* [*obliged*] to maintain many more people than I." They insisted however in order that he *should avail himself* [*should will to profit*] of a portion at least of that money: "*If* you wish thus," added the philosopher, "in sign of gratitude I will accept thirty *minæ*[2]." He took the value of fifteen of our livres, and dismissed them with the remainder.

[1] lo rimetterete. [2] mine.

---

81. THE MERITED RECOMPENSE DIVERTED TO ANOTHER.[1]

In 1707, the squadrons of M. M. Forbin and Duguay-Trouin joined each other, *gave* [*presented*] battle to the English and remained victors. The last, always equal to himself, did prodigies of valour. Louis XIV, who *was constantly bestowing benefits on him* [*ceased not to benefit him*][2], having-heard of this victory, assigned to him a pension of a thousand livres. Duguay-Trouin wrote to the minister, supplicating him to *be so kind as to* [*will to*] interest himself with the Sovereign to the end that he should be pleased to turn this benefit to favour of M. Saint-Huban, *the next in command to him* [*his captain in second*], who had remained wounded in the combat, and who had much more need than he of succour, assuring him that he thought himself even too much recompensed if he could procure advantages to his officers. The minister respected his desire, and the captain *obtained*[3] the pension in place to the commander.

[1] rivolta ad altri.   [2] beneficarlo.   [3] conseguì.

[2] *To benefit* is often, as we have seen, giovare; beneficare is a synonymous term, but less general in its use, and chiefly employed when the *benefit* is a *gift*.   [3] Not buscò, which would imply that the captain had *made efforts* to obtain it.

---

82. The Mistake of a Cipher[1].

At Rome, a woman, whose poverty was in part compensated by the consolation of possessing a daughter embellished by those modest graces which are indications of natural *wisdom*[2], presented herself with this young woman to the Cardinal Farnese, and with a *piteous*[3] air narrated to him how she was about to be *ousted*[4] from a *corner*[5] which she *rented*[6] in the house of a rich person, through not being able to pay him a *balance*[7] of five crowns. The Cardinal wrote a note, and consigned it to the suppliant, *instructing*[8] her to present it to his steward. The latter, *having read it* [*read that he had it*], counted to her at once fifty crowns. "Sir," said the woman, "His Eminence has certainly *made the mistake* [*mistaken*] of a nought, because I have asked of him but five crowns, and he through error *must have* [*will have*] written fifty." *As she refused on any terms* [*Refusing she at every condition*][9] to receive this sum, the agent found himself constrained to present himself to his master whereby to have an elucidation on *this matter* [*such article*].

The Cardinal took back the note: "It is true," he said,
"I have precisely *made the mistake* of a nought, and
the honesty of that poor woman manifests it to me."
He added a nought to the fifty, and ordered that five
hundred crowns should be counted to her.

¹zero. ²saggezza. ³compassionevole. ⁴scacciata. ⁵angolo.
⁶teneva a pigione. ⁷avanzo. ⁸avvertendola. ⁹patto.

² The Fr. *sagesse,* wise and right conduct. ⁹ Literally, *covenant,*
agreement.

83. THE AMENDMENT ¹.

A private person lived tranquilly with his family
on [*in*] a little farm of which the moderate income
being every year absorbed by the indispensable expenses, *nothing remained over* [*there did not remain over
to him*] *wherewith*² to improve the *land* [*lands*].
M. Sabz, his friend, offered himself, to this effect, to
assist him with a loan, payable *at* [*in*] three diverse
times. *Being-received*³ willingly the offer, the most
grateful debtor made three *payables*⁴ to M. Sabz.

The *profit* [*fruit*] not corresponding to the sum
employed in the improvements, *it followed thence*⁵
that the debtor, at the epoch of the two first *fallings-
due*⁶, found himself much embarrassed; nevertheless,
*straitening himself to the utmost*⁷, he *met* [*satisfied*]
both. In all this tract of time the two persons continued to be intimate friends; but being-arrived the
day of withdrawing the third note of hand⁸, the debtor
perceived himself to be in absolute powerlessness to do

it, wherefore, instead of having recourse to ruinous
means, *depending* [*leaning*] on the cordial friendship
that between them subsisted, and considering the spon-
taneity of the offer and the *failure* [*uselessness*] of its
effect, having-overcome every repugnance, he revealed
to M. Sabz his circumstances, and prayed him for a
delay. The request was granted him, *rudely*[9] however
and with certain *muttered hints* [*maimed words*][10],
from which it seemed that the creditor accused the
other of culpable carelessness.

The latter, stung by such unexpected *demeanour*[11],
sought at every cost money, and *obtained it*[12]. *The
moment it was* [*Scarcely was it*] in his power, he
sent it to M. Sabz, notifying to him to restore to him
the last of his *bonds*[8]. It is easy to foresee that,
after this step, he who reputed himself offended *considered himself dispensed* [*supposed to be dispensed*]
from every *attention*[13] towards the other; and behold
two *old* [*ancient*] friends break off every correspondence,
and have nothing more *in* [*of*] common between them.

In such a state of things, *it was not long before
M. Sabz perceived himself to be in the wrong* [*delayed
not M. Sabz to know his own wrong*], and thought
seriously about the mode of repairing it. So many
were his secret researches, till *he attained*[14] to discover
the person who had lent the money to the offended.
He repaired to him, paid him entirely, had back from
him the *bond*[8], and prayed him to *conceal the whole*[15]
from his debtor until he should present himself to *pay*
[*satisfy*] him.

Being-passed five months, went the latter to extinguish the debt, and *received for* [*had in*] answer:
"*You long ago ceased, Sir, to owe me It is from*

much time, O Sir, that you owe not to me more] anything; M. Sabz has already paid me for you."

What a revolution at such words in the spirit of the debtor! *Laying aside every other feeling [Being-abandoned whatsoever regard]*, he flew to his friend, testified to him his lively gratitude and presented to him the money. The latter, at the *summit*[16] of his desires in again seeing him *appeased*[17], embraced him, they kissed each other, nor would he receive that sum, *asserting it [saying]* to be a just thing that he should bear the penalty of his *churlish conduct*[18], and *himself to be too happy a man [to hold himself for too fortunate]* if he could reunite at that price knots so dear to his heart. But the friend showed himself resolved not to will to receive the gift, and here *sprang up* a new contest, very different however from the first, which was *settled [composed]* by the unanimous assent that that money should pass to the daughter of the debtor, and should serve to augment her dowry.

[1]ravvedimento. [2]di che. [3]accolta. [4]pagherò. [5]ne avvenne. [6]scadenze. [7]ristringendosi possibilmente. [8]chirografo. [9]sgarbatamente. [10]tronche parole. [11]contegno. [12]ne rinvenne. [13]officiosità. [14]giunse. [15]occultare il tutto. [16]colmo. [17]placato. [18]inurbano procedere.

[1]The idea conveyed by ravvedimento is, coming to *see* things in a truer light. [6]Scadere = to expire = to fall due. [8]Precisely our *note of hand*; the Ital. is derived from the Greek. [9]Garbo (whence garbato, sgarbato &c.) is pretty nearly our *grace*. "Fatelo con garbo, con bel garbo = do it gracefully, delicately. — Vedrete che lo farà con mal garbo, = you will see he will do it with an ill grace. — Che garbo è questo? = What way of behaving is this?" [10]Troncare = to cut short = truncate. [13]From the same root as our *officious*, which is always used in a bad sense; whereas

officioso = ready with good *offices* = obliging. [15]We have the adj. *occult*, and the noun *occultation*, but not the verb. [17]We have the adj. *placable*. [18]Urbano = urbane, from the Latin *urbs*, a city; as civile = civil, is from *cives*, a citizen. The idea in both is of course the greater refinement and courtesy practised in the social life of cities.

84. The good Porter of Milan.

In the year 1779, a porter, at Milan, found by chance a bag in which were two hundred crowns, and *had bills posted up* [*made affix the advertisements of it*] through the city. The proprietor of it appeared, who, *having described it* [*given of it the marks*] had back immediately his crowns, from whose number he *took*[1] twenty and offered them in recompense to the porter. The latter refused them in such wise that he made the owner of the bag *suspect* [*doubt*][2] that to be perhaps too mean an offer; wherefore he carried it even to [*the*] thirty. Having had a repulse yet more resolute, he comprehended at last that the worthy man did not want recompense, at the which *provoked*[3], he threw the bag on the ground saying: "If you hinder me from showing you my gratitude, I have not lost anything, and the bag will remain here." It was then that the good porter *made up his mind* [*determined*] to take five crowns, saying *he would take* [*to carry*] them at once *as a* [*in*] gift to a poor family, of which, for greater security, he *revealed*[4] also the name.

[1]tolse. [3]indispettito. [4]palesò.

[2] Dubitare is frequently = to suspect, to fear. [3] From dispetto (Fr. *dépit*).

85. THE HEIR THROUGH COMPASSION.

The celebrated M. de la Martinière, *head [first]*
surgeon of Louis XVI, by the exercise of his profession *became so rich [enriched in such wise]*, that, dying
intestate, he left an inheritance of a million and half
of livres. No one presenting himself *as the legal [in
quality of necessary]* heir, the money and the movea-
bles were consigned in deposit to a notary, charged
to search if there were any person who had a right to
the inheritance [such succession].

*The advertisements of it having-been caused to be
printed in the public papers*[1], four peasants presented
themselves, and placed under the eye of the notary
the titles on which they founded their pretensions.
He, *having first made*[2] a mature examination, decided
that three of them had a right to the inheritance; but
a fourth, through being more distant in *relationship*[3]
by one grade, could not aspire to it. *This poor man,
disappointed in his hope [Being-remained disappointed
in his hope this unhappy]*, deplored his own fate and
the expenses *incurred [met]* for the long journey. If
before, not *flattered by hopes of a*[4] possible change,
he suffered patiently a condition to which he was
accustomed[5], this became to him then insupportable;
and comparing the state to which he saw the others
raised with the indigence to which he found himself
condemned, *his life became a burden to him [turned
out to him heavy and tormenting the life]*. But as he
could not complain of injustice committed to his hurt,
so all the signs of his *regret*[6] reduced themselves to
tears.

The three companions *were* [*remained*] *deeply*[7]
moved : compassion imposed silence *on self-interest* [*to
interest*] in their heart and *spoke eloquently in*[8] favour
of that unfortunate. They took *then*[9] the resolution
not to let him depart in such *adness*[10], and council
held between them, they *determined* to *give him a share*[11]
of the inheritance. When they heard from the notary
that even from that moment nothing opposed itself to
the execution of their project, they ceded to him a
hundred and sixty thousand livres, and excused themselves *to* [*with*] him for not being able to do more,
alleging *as their* [*in*] motive the succour that they
must lend to other *poor* [*mean*][12] persons, to whom
also they were bound with the ties of blood.

[1]essendosene fatti stampare gli avvisi su' fogli pubblici.
[2]premesso. [3]parentela. [4]lusingato da. [5]avvezzo. [6]rincrescimento.
[7]al sommo. [8]perorò a. [9]quindi. [10]contristamento. [11]metterlo
a parte. [12]meschine.

[1]Newspapers and broad sheets are fogli, not carte. [5]Avvezzo,
adj.; avvezzato, part. Why is the adj. right here? [10]From tristo.
[12]This adj. does not here imply contempt: it is simply = of *mean*
or *low* estate.

86. The Viscount de Turenne.

It suffices not to do good, but it is necessary likewise to know how to do it. *Gifts lavished indiscriminately* [*Profusions, shed indistinctly*] *may* [*can*] even
feed vice and *idleness*[1] to the hurt of the helpless poor
and of *society at large* [*all the society*]*: one may*[2]
benefit through ostentation, one may *publish*[3] the

benefit, exalt its worth, do it rudely, accompanied by
stinging and mortifying words, an account of [*for*] which
an unhappy one may blush, be saddened, be irritated
to see himself constrained by want to receive the gift.
A beautiful thing is giving and hiding the hand, and
more beautiful yet behaving oneself in such wise that
the benefactor seem on the contrary the benefited: one
cannot do good with greater delicacy than this.

Few can be compared to the Marshal Viscount de
Turenne in this nobility of benefaction. *Having dis-*
covered [*coming he to discover*] that some regiment of
the army, of which he had the command, was in grave
disorder, and this not *indeed*[4] through negligence of
the captains, but through effect of the poverty into which
they were fallen, he feigned that the King had sent
him money, and instead dispensed *what belonged to*
himself [*that of his right*], to the end that in those
bodies [*corps of army*] order should be immediately
re-established.

He *one day learned* [*came one day to know*] that
a poor officer was almost desperate through having lost
two horses in an *affair*[5] of arms. He *sent for him*
[*called him to himself*], and obliged him to take two
of his on condition that he *said not a* [*should not make*]
word to any one of this gift: "If you tell it," he
added, "other officers too will come to ask some of
me, and I am not in *a condition* [*grade*] to *give*[6]
to all."

More courteously still he bore himself with another
military-man of birth very distinguished, but poor and
very ill *equipped* [*in harness*]. The Viscount sought
so many occasions to *confer*[7] casually with him, that
at last *he succeeded* in finding one. "Sir," he said to

him, "I have to make a *request*[8] to you; I do *indeed*[4]
foresee that it will *seem* [*turn out*] to you somewhat
bold, I will nevertheless flatter myself that you will
not let escape you this occasion to *confer an obligation
on* [*render to you obliged*] your general. I am old
and suffer now some *infirmities*[9]: horses too lively tire
me. I saw you by chance one day on yours, and it
appeared to me that it would much have suited me.
Provided that *the sacrifice in question be not* [*it treats
not, my dear, of a sacrifice*] too great for you, *I beg*
[*I am to pray*] you to cede it to me, for I in exchange
will give you one of mine." The officer answered
with a profound reverence, and having-taken his horse,
which might be worth five louis, led him at once with
his own hand to the stable of the Marshal, who the
day following sent to him instead one of his best, which
cost at least ten times more.

[1]poltroneria. [2]si può. [3]decantare. [4]già. [5]fatto. [6]regalarne. [7]abboccarsi. [8]istanza. [9]acciacchi.

[8]This word implies urgency; as we say "to pray *instantly*,'
and the Fr. "prier *instamment*, avec *instance*; faire des *instances*."

87. The generous Creditor.

In London, the celebrated Garrick *lent* [*gave on
loan*] five hundred pounds sterling to a man esteemed
generally for his probity. Some time being-elapsed,
the latter found himself in danger of failing through
fault of his debtors. His *luckless*[1] situation moved his
relations and friends, who resolved one day to *meet*

[*convoke themselves*] to *contrive* [*combine*] the means to
draw him from embarrassment [2]. The news of such a
conference reached to the ears of Garrick, who in
place of *availing himself of it* [3] to secure the fate of
his own credit, *folded* [4] in a letter the *security* [5], and
directed it to that assembly. The letter was of the
following tenor:

"It was told me, O Sirs, that today you are
gathered as good friends. Truly I also would have
wished to assist at this festival. *Though* [*If*] I have
not received of it the invitation, permit me at least *to
have part in it as best I can* [6]. *I imagine* [*figure to
myself*] that you will make a good dinner; and since
the cold is very great, you will light also a beautiful
fire. *Accept* [7], I pray you, the enclosed paper which
will serve to *kindle* [*excite*] it."

[1] infausta. [2] trarlo d'impaccio. [3] prevalersene. [4] ne compiegò.
[5] cauzione. [6] che ne sia a parte come meglio per me si può.
[7] aggradite.

88. Boileau and Catherine II.

Patru, *called* [1] the Quintilian of France, was *sued
at law* [*pressed* [2] *by the forensic acts*] for a debt of
four thousand livres *to* [*towards*] the Receiver General
of the finances. Not knowing by what other means to
free himself from such importunity, he determined to
sell his library. The celebrated Boileau, who was not
rich, having-heard the unhappy state of the respectable
lawyer [3], presented himself to him to make its *purchase*,
and offered him a price greater than that which the

11

proprietor asked. Having-done this, he prayed him to *take care of*[4] the books which he had bought, and in recompense of such custody left to him the free use of them for all his life.

More generously still behaved towards the philosopher Diderot the empress Catherine II. She bought his library, and having-disbursed its price, entrusted it to his custody, as long as he lived; nor *satisfied with this*[5], she assigned to him a pension in quality of her *librarian*[6].

---

[1] detto.　[2] incalzato.　[3] giureconsulto.　[4] custodire.　[5] di ciò paga.　[6] bibliotecario.

[1] Far more idiomatic than chiamato in reference to this kind of surname.　[4] So the guardian of a museum, &c. is called the custode.

---

89. The noble Recompense.

At Turin, a *gentleman*[1] of consideration having suffered the most cruel blows from fortune, saw himself constrained to renounce that splendour with which until that *moment* [*point*] he had maintained his family. In the imparting to his wife the *lamentable* [*tearful*] state of his own affairs, he talked to her with a *frankness*[2] and a *good grace* such *as to soften* [*that it softened*] in the heart of that lady the pain which must bring to her a similar announcement. "My dear," he said to her, "I have *dispossessed*[3] myself of all that which fate permitted me to possess when she was propitious to me, and I cannot dispense myself from praying you also to follow in this my example. *Hence-forward*[4] our family must be reduced to a man-servant and to a cook. I know that you have a maid whom you love much, and it is *on this account* [*for this*] that I cannot beg of you the sacrifice of her except with my much grief; this sacrifice is however indispensable, and I flatter myself that you will not refuse it me."

However cruel such a separation was to the lady, nevertheless having-seen its necessity, she sought to adapt herself to it. *She sent for*[5] the maid, and communicated to her her resolution, without hiding from her how painful was this separation [*detachment*] to her heart. "Madam," answered her the young woman, "it is known to you that I have some ability; it seems to me impossible, *if* you would permit me to remain with you, that my *little wit*[6] could not suffice me to supply the expenses of my subsistence. Deign then to consider me as *on board*[7]: all the time of which I shall be able to dispose will be for you: nor *do I expect* [*pretend*] other *guerdon*[8], O Madam, except the felicity to be beside you." Such words made weep both, and they separated without concluding anything.

The *gentleman* heard the tenor of this conference. *At the end of* [*Being-passed*] half an hour, a servant announces to the lady that *dinner is served* [*the table*[9] *is already in readiness*]. The master passes *into the servants' hall*[10] and commands that there be placed on the table a third *cover*[11] — "Expect you some *stranger*[12]?" says to him his wife. "No Madam," responds the *gentleman*: "make descend the maid." This young-woman is called; she descends, and the master *goes up to her*[13], takes her by the hand and *leads* [*approaches*]

11*

her to the table: "Madam," he says to her, "the nobility of your sentiments renders you equal to us, and
the sensibility of your heart makes you our common
friend for ever. Take place at our *side*[14]: *henceforward*[4] you will have none other than this."

Providence *caused* [*did so*] that so noble and delicate
a manner of recompensing a *noble* [*beautiful*] heart
should *soon* [*in brief*] have its *guerdon*[8]. There *elapsed*[15]
not two years before this *noble* [*egregious*] family had
again all its ancient splendour.

[1] cavaliere. [2] disinvoltura. [3] spropriato. [4] d'ora innanzi, d'ora
in poi. [5] fece chiamare. [6] piccolo ingegno. [7] in pensione. [8] mer-
cede, guiderdone. [9] mensa. [10] in tinello. [11] posata. [12] forestiere.
[13] se le fa incontro. [14] fianco. [15] trascorsero.

[1] The title given to the younger son of a noble house; corresponding to our "Honourable." — In mediæval language cavaliere
is of course knight; nor is there any other term to represent a
modern English knight's title. Baronet is baronetto. [2] Involvere
= to involve = wrap up; disinvoltura is therefore = freedom
from involved phrases = straightforward speech. [3] From proprio.
[5] A very common idiom. — "Chiamate *or* fate chiamare il medico
= send for the physician." [7] Like the French. [9] Because it is a
table for a meal. [11] From posare, = to *lay* the table.

---

90. The Captain of Algiers.

Louis XIV, indignant *at* [*of*] the faithlessness and
the arrogance of the Algerines, commanded Duquesne
to bombard Algiers. The general gave order to the
fleet to approach, *in spite of*[1] the fire incessant and
terrible of the enemy: and when he saw it at a suita-

ble interval, he made *fall*[2] on the city a hail of bombs and of balls. The enemy having in vain employed every effort to repulse this attack, in place of suspending the defence and of proposing a capitulation, heard only the voice of his fury, and *resorted*[3] to such a project as could not *certainly enter the head* [*fall certainly into thought*] except *of* [*to*] men barbarous and inhuman. *These people invented the plan*[4] to attach to the mouth of all their cannons a French slave, *in such a way*[5] that the fleet of the besiegers was not so much by the balls hit, as by the *torn*[6] limbs of their deplorable compatriots.

In such moments of horror it happened that an Algerine captain, who had been prisoner in France for some time and had received there a most humane *reception*[7], recognised, among the victims destined to this ferocious *slaughter*[8], an officer from whom he had received very singular favours. He *immediately interested himself most strongly in his favour* [*took at once a lively interest*[9] *for him*]; much he prayed and much offered to save his life: but brutality has not ears. Perceiving that all was useless, and that his friend *was being hung*[10] to the mouth of the cannon *to do him to fragments, as if transported out of*[11] himself, he threw himself on his neck, clasped him between his arms, and turning himself to the cannonier: "*Fire*[12]," he cried: if I cannot save a benefactor of mine, I will at least have the satisfaction of dying with him." The Dey, present at this act of magnanimous gratitude, *was* [*remained*] vividly struck with it, and *for the sake* [*in grace*] of so heroic a resolution granted to the captain that which he had refused to his prayers and offers.

¹in onta al. ²piombare. ³appigliossi. ⁴immaginarono costoro.
⁵di modo. ⁶squarciate. ⁷accoglimento. ⁸carnificina. ⁹impegno.
¹⁰si stava appendendo. ¹¹per farlo a brani, rapito come a. ¹²tira.

¹⁰Not impiccando, which would imply strangling. ¹²Tirare =
far fuoco = to let off = to fire.

91. Mercy remunerated.

In the Seven Years' War, a Prussian hussar, after a
combat, encountered on the field of battle a young
officer enemy seriously wounded, who prayed him to
put an end to his sufferings by taking from him the
little life which remained to him. "*No indeed [This
then no]*," answered the hussar, "God guard me from
it. I will carry thee rather to the hospital, where thou
canst perhaps *be cured [cure]*." Thus did the good
man, and the wounded one *by the end of*¹ two months
recovered himself perfectly.

Full of gratitude towards his benefactor, whom he
had never *lost sight of*², he offered him as much as
he had to recompense him; every proffer was however
vain, *as it seemed [seeming]* to the good Prussian to be
recompensed enough by the *mere [same]* humanity of
the action. Nevertheless, to liberate himself from the
importunity of this youth who was always *hovering
about him [at his shoulders]*, he consented at last to
accept a watch, as a memorial of that which had passed
between them.

Peace made, the regiment in which the hussar
served, *was disbanded [came dissolved]*; and he found
himself without employment. Not knowing to what

course to resort, *there came [mounted]* into his head to transfer himself into Hungary, and to exercise there the business of *breaker-in*[3] of horses. There he was presented to Prince Esterhazy, who wished to have one of them in his service. When he saw this man, he wondered, and asked him if he had served in quality of soldier in the Seven Years' War, and if he had ever saved the life of some officer enemy. "Perhaps of more than one," answered the Prussian, and *certainly of him [of that-one then certainly]* who has given me this watch." — "I am," resumed the Prince, "he who has given it you; it is I who owe you my life. God has sent you here in order that I *might [could]* testify to you my gratitude." What surprise for that veteran! The issue was that he created him his first *equerry*[4], kept him always at his side; lived familiarly with him, nor ceased through all his life to give him the most affectionate marks of gratitude.

[1] in capo a. [2] perduto di vista. [3] dirozzatore. [4] scudiere.

[3] From rozzo = rough, untrained.

92. CLAUDE FAVRE.

In the year 1619, Louis XIII assigned a pension of two thousand francs to Claude Favre, a French *literary-man*[1], in order that he also might concur *in [to]* the work of the Dictionary of the Royal Academy. *Before long [Passed not much that]* his pension *was* suspended; and he, following the ordinary lot of *lite-*

rary men [persons of letters], fell into deplorable poverty. The Cardinal de Richelieu, condescending to
the *importunities* [2] of those who spoke to him in his
favour, *restored [re-established]* it to him; and when
the literary-man *came [repaired]* to thank him for the
favour obtained, the Minister smiling said to him:
"You thus will *certainly* not forget in the Dictionary
the *word* [3] *pension.*" — "No, *Monseigneur,* [4]" answered
at once le Favre, "and much less the other, *gratitude.*"

[1] letterato. [2] istanze. [3] voce. [4] monsignore.

93. THE INGENIOUS GRATITUDE.

A distinguished personage of Paris was crossing
the Seine, between the Invalides and the Pont Royal,
and in the boat which transported him *was [found
herself]* also a woman of the people who was making
the same *passage* [1]. He, to pass the time, asked her
if she were married. — "Yes, sir," she answered. —
"And where do you live?" he added. — "At Gros-
Caillou." — "Whither are you *bound [directed]* at
present?" — "I go to the barrier of Roulle, to buy
bread." — "Are there *then no [not perhaps]* vendors
of bread at Gros-Caillou, without going so far?" —
There are *plenty [right well]* [2] of them." — "At the
Roulle *I suppose it is [it will be]* better, is it not true?
or cheaper?" — "Oh, no sir." — "Why then go *so
far as* [3] there?" — "Because, before my husband had
an employment, we were miserable; the baker who
resides at present at the Roulle *lived then near us* [4],
and had the kindness to give us bread *on credit* [5].

Now we have *a little property*[6], and gratitude *requires* [*wills*] that we buy *for cash*[7] our bread from him, *since once*[8] he has used the charity of waiting for his money."

[1]tragitto. [2]benissimo. [3]sin. [4]ci stava allora dappresso. [5]in credenza. [6]un po' di roba. [7]a contanti. [8]posto che un tempo.

[1]Fr. *trajet.* [6]This elision is very frequent in *poco.* [7]Danari contanti = ready money (in Fr. also *argent comptant*).

---

94. The Florentine Shoemaker.

At Florence, a lady who belonged to a distinguished family, sustaining for *several* [*more*] years a *lawsuit*[1] against *her* [*one her*] brother-in-law, was reduced to such straitened fortune, that sometimes she lacked even *things of absolute* [*objects of first*] necessity. One day came her shoemaker to ask of her money, and she, having to send him away empty, *underwent from him*[2] some rudeness. *While* [*In the act that*] with fair words she sought to soften him, wanting to persuade him that her creditors were much at her heart; that she expected in *a short time* [*brief*] money; that he would *be* [*have been*] amongst the first to share it, that *clownish*[3] man cast *from time to time* his eyes on a *hearth*[4] that he saw extinct, although on a day very cold. This circumstance began to occupy him, and he let escape him between the teeth: "The marchioness *is* not cold *on* [*in*] days of this *sort* [*make*][5]*!*" — "Oh, I am indeed," she *frankly*[6] answered; "but if *fuel*[7] is wanting, how does one to warm oneself?" The shoe-

maker *stood awhile irresolute*[8]*:* it appeared that he
wanted to say some other thing, but that the fear of
offending the marchioness restrained him, and he took
leave.

She, the day following, perceived that two carts
had drawn up[9] at the house-door, and asked of the
servant-maid the *reason* [*motive*]. "Madam," she answered, "they are two carts of wood for you." Not
believing it [*lending to it faith*], *she sent for*[10] the
carters, and having-heard that they had received the
order to *unload them*[11] in her house without saying a
word, she *maintained* [*sustained*] that this was not
possible, and that certainly they had mistaken the door.
They were therefore constrained to return to the shoemaker's and to induce him, if he wanted to *carry out
his* [*obtain the*] intent, *himself to repair to the marchioness' house.*

The poor man, extremely confused, was almost
about to throw himself at her feet. "Madam," he said
to her," pardon me, for pity's sake, *so great*[12] boldness:
believe me, in truth, it is not indeed to offend you that
I have done this; but my compassion was so much
yesterday at seeing a lady of such high degree half
dead from the cold, that I have not been able to
restrain myself from executing this project. Of course
I intend not *at all*[13] to make you a gift of this wood:
you will pay me for it together with the shoes, immediately *you succeed in drawing*[14] money; but, I pray
you, accept them . . . . I am a *clown*[15], see; but yet
I have a good heart . . ." And here began to *escape
him*[16] some tears.

The lady surprised and affected: "Yes, yes, my
friend," she answered, *"be easy* [*remain tranquil*], I

profess to you *on the contrary*[17] very much obligation.
I *buy* from you this wood, and hope to pay you for
it very quickly; I reserve to myself to a better time
the pleasure of making you know how great is my
gratitude."

Being-passed some months, the marchioness gained
the lawsuit and *regained her prosperity* [*gave back to
prosperous state her fortune*]. Mindful of the benefit,
she delayed not to write to the shoemaker the following note:

Friend, I blush not to acknowledge you for my benefactor: I will *on the contrary*[17] that all know it.
None of those who come into my house *had noticed*[18]
that fuel was wanting on the hearth; you alone perceived it in order to diminish my *straitnesses*[19]. I
shall be most grateful to you *so long as*[20] I shall have
life. Awaiting the moment to *acquit* [*comport*] myself
better *towards* [*with*] you, I have given meanwhile
commission to my *servant*[21] to pay you for the fuel
and the shoes. Come to see me: I will seek to be
useful to you and to your family.

This note was authenticated by the signature, a
thing which another lady would perhaps have *deemed*[22]
better to *omit*[23]. The servant consigned to the shoemaker three hundred sequins. "Here there is certainly
a mistake," said the good man, "since I think to be
barely[24] creditor for four." — "The marchioness,"
answered smiling the servant, "is not used to pay less
that quality of fuel:" he had received order to answer thus.

The artisan presented himself at the palace to return
thanks to the lady, and to *congratulate her on the*[25]
lawsuit which she had gained. The latter welcomed

him with the most lively demonstrations of gratitude, and presented him to those who then *were* with her, narrating to them with the heart strongly moved the generous action of the poor shoemaker.

[1]lite. [2]ne riporto. [3]zotico. [4]focolare. [5]fatta. [6]schietta-mente. [7]le legne. [8]stette alquanto sospeso. [9]eransi fermate. [10]fece venire a se. [11]scaricarle. [12]un tanto. [13]mica. [14]vi verrà fatto di riscuoter. [15]omaccio. [16]sfuggirgli. [17]anzi. [18]si era av-veduto. [19]angustie. [20]finchè. [21]cameriere. [22]stimato. [23]sor-passare. [24]appena. [25]congratularsi con lei della.

[7]Legno, pl. legni, wood in general. Legna both sing. and pl., and legne pl., wood to burn. Legno can also be used for wood to burn, but legna is to be preferred. [12]In like manner un tant' uomo, so great a man; un tanto poeta, so great a poet. [23]Sor-passare = sopra-passare = to pass over = to omit. [25]Note this construction.

95. The Soldier through gratitude.

In the year 1762, an *infant*[1] by name Peter, who belonged to the hospital of the *foundlings*[2] of Paris, was consigned to a *nurse*[3] of Saint-Quentin in order that she might *nurse* [*nourish*] him. Arrived at the age of five years, the pious place had him again; but this child, to whom that sojourn turned out insuffera-ble, found the means to flee and to return again to his Saint-Quentin. A pastrycook, taking pity on the misery to which he *perceived*[4] him reduced in the house of his *destitute*[5] *nurse*[3], received him into his own, clothed him, maintained him and taught to him his trade. Peter grew and *attached himself*[6] to his bene-factor in such wise that he would have given his life for him.

It happened one day that a creditor of the pastrycook *exacted of a sudden*⁷ the payment of a sum to which, although not excessive, nevertheless the debtor was not in *a condition [grade]* at once to satisfy. To *get out of [draw himself from]* this perplexity, he resolved to sell a portion of his *plate*⁸, and to *this*⁹ effect, *having confided [confided that he had]* to his faithful Peter the *strait [urgency]* in which he found himself, he charged him with the sale of it.

The latter, supremely sensible of the disorder of the affairs of his beloved master, *thought of [imagined]* a strange expedient *whereby to remedy it*¹⁰. He begged him to defer for a moment the execution of the adopted measure, and repaired to M. de Fransure, colonel of the royal corps of artillery, to whom he gave his name to serve in quality of *a common*¹¹ soldier.

Having-drawn the price of the enlisting, he ran to carry it to his benefactor: "Take," he said; "*I have long desired [it is long time that I desire]* to serve my King: this money will suffice to the payment of the debt, without that you be obliged to sell the plate." The master surprised and moved tried in vain to constrain the youth to regard as his that sum; there was not a thing capable of *moving him*¹² from the taken course. Being-informed of this his regiment, it charged itself *with having him taught* to read and to write, at its own expenses, to the end that he might one day become an officer.

---

¹bambino. ²esposti. ³balia, nutrice. ⁴scorgea. ⁵mendica. ⁶si affezionò. ⁷esigesse d'improvviso. ⁸argenteria. ⁹tal. ¹⁰onde porvi riparo. ¹¹semplice. ¹²smuoverlo.

174

¹²Muovere = to *move* in general; commuovere = to *move* the heart; smuovere, here = to *move* the mind or will, is synonymous with both the others, but usually implies difficulty.

96. THE MERCHANT ENNOBLED.

Louis XI, always *greedy of information*[1], invited to his table foreigners, when he flattered himself to *draw from them*[2] some useful *piece of knowledge*[3]; nor disdained he to welcome amongst this number also some merchant who *might have supplied*[4] to him lights concerning commerce, trusting that the freedom of the granted table would have engaged him to speak familiarly with him.

One of these merchants, *letting his fancy become heated*[5] by such *courtesies*[6] of the King his lord, bethought himself to crave of him letters of nobility. Louis consented to it, but *always whenever*[7] the new nobleman appeared in his presence, the Monarch feigned not to be aware of him, and scarcely directed to him a look. Stung to the quick by such unwonted demeanour, the poor man could not dissemble, one day, the lively displeasure that he experienced thereby; of which the Sovereign *having-become aware*[8]: "Sir gentleman, be not surprised thereat," he said to him: "When I invited you to table, you were regarded by me among the first of your order: now you are become the last of that in which it pleased you to *reckon yourself*[9]; and it would be doing an injury to the *ancient*[10] nobles, if I continued to *distinguish you as before* [*use towards you the distinctions which I did practise towards you*]."

¹avído d'istruírsi. ²ritrarne. ³cognizione. ⁴avesse somminí-
strato. ⁵lasciandosi riscaldar la fantasia. ⁶gentilezze. ⁷ogni qual
volta. ⁸fatto accorto. ⁹ascrivervi. ¹⁰anziani.

¹Avido and ingordo are both *greedy;* but the former only can
be used in a good sense. — Istruirsi — to learn, obtain information; una persona istruita = a well-informed person. ³From
cognoscere, an old form of conoscere; hence also cognito and in-
cognito. ⁴Qualche — che, commonly takes the subjunctive. — The
idea here is that though you may invite a person from whom you
expect information, you cannot be sure that he will furnish it till
you have tried. ⁸Literally "having become aware by perceiving."
¹⁰Anziano implies seniority, and must not be confounded with
antico.

97. The Rivalries¹ between Demosthenes and Æschines.

It was on the occasion of declaiming against Philip
the Macedonian that Æschines made himself known,
one of the first orators whom Greece has had. The
Athenian Republic deputed him as envoy to this prince,
and the gold of Philip changed the violent declaimer
into the most *mild*² of men. Demosthenes his rival
accused him as *one*³ who sacrificed to his own interest
the public weal; and Æschines would have had to
succumb if the credit of Eubulus had not saved him.

Having-elapsed some time, it happened that the
people decreed a crown of gold to Demosthenes.
Æschines *rose up*⁴ against this decree; indeed to
assure himself *yet more*⁵ of *bringing it to nought*
[*sending it to void*], following the prescribed formalities,
he accused Ctesiphon, as him who had proposed such
a gift. And it was on such occassion that the two
rivals recited those discourses which would be a master-

piece of eloquence, if they were not debased by the dishonourable insults which reciprocally *hurled against each other*[6] the orators. In this *conflict [wrestling-match]*[7] Æschines remained *overcome*[8], and was condemned to exile.

He was going out of Athens, when Demosthenes, *following [keeping behind]* his steps with a purse of money in his hand, overtook him, gave to him the most lively marks of sincere benevolence and obliged him to accept it. This unexpected conduct *on part of a rival*[9] who had been by him acrimoniously persecuted, made a strong impression on the spirit of the unhappy Orator: "And how must not I deplore," said he then, with the tears in his eyes, "the loss of a native-land, in which I leave an enemy *so*[10] generous, that it is not *to be hoped*[11] that I should find elsewhere a friend who resembles him!"

Such sentiments towards his magnanimous competitor never cancelled themselves from his spirit. Having-established himself at Rhodes, he opened a school of eloquence whereby to have *the means of living [of what to live]*, and gave beginning to his lessons by reading the two harangues which had caused his exile. *When he had finished [Terminated that he had]* his, the hearers failed not to lavish on him praises; but when *afterwards*[12] he finished to read that of Demosthenes, they passed on to enthusiasm, and the acclamations *seemed as if they would never stop [were never ceasing]:* "Ah dear friends," exclaimed then Æschines, more magnanimous still in this circumstance than his rival, "what then would it have been if you had heard it recited by his mouth?"

¹ gare. ² mansueto. ³ quegli. ⁴ insorse. ⁵ vieppiù. ⁶ si
scagliarono. ⁷ lotta. ⁸ succumbente. ⁹ per parte d'un emulo.
¹⁰ cotanto. ¹¹ sperabile. ¹² poi.

² Also used of animals to signify *tame*. ³ Quegli points out a
definite person. ⁴ Used of *moral* rising up. ⁵ A very usual expression; sometimes written *vie più*. ⁷ Fr. *lutte*. ¹¹ The root? ¹² Poi
scarcely relates to time or order here; it is an expletive.

98. How one should¹ die.

Phocion was such a general that Greece fortyfive
times entrusted to him her armies: he always drew
victory *after* [*behind*] his steps. Cassander, one of the
successors of Alexander the Macedonian, jealous of so
much glory, accused him in face of the people, not
being-ignorant of the art to prepossess them *in* [*to*] his
own favour.

Phocion presents himself to the seduced assembly
with that intrepidity which the testimony of a *stainless*²
conscience inspires, and with that air noble and frank
which beseems a man who has rendered signal services
to his country. Scarcely however he *uncloses*³ his
mouth whereby to pronounce his defence, *a hollow
'murmur*⁴, which goes gradually growing and transforms
itself into a general tumult, makes him comprehend
what [*thing*] he· must expect from a people inconsiderate, ungrateful, *volatile*⁵, corrupted by the promises
and by the gold of his enemy. For the which thing,
convinced of the inutility of all that which he could
have said in his own justification, he *subsides* [*puts
himself*] into silence, and having-seized a moment in
which the assembly has *become* [*made itself*] less tu-

12

multuous, not other grace he asks than a just pity towards those who *are* regarded as his accomplices, and *whom it was wished to involve*[6] in his irreparable misfortune.

Being-terminated this prayer, he was reconducted into prison, followed by the infamous *train*[7] of his accusers, and girt by a crowd of people greedy always of this *kind* [*quality*] of spectacles. On the road *there was some one who went so far as even*[8] to spit in his face: nor for this was moved the hero, but *limited himself*[9] to say only: "Is there not any among you who will impede to this man to commit actions so *foul*[10]?"

When he was arrived at the prison, he took *intrepidly* [*intrepid*] the *bowl*[11] which contained the *hemlock*[12]. Before he approached it to his mouth, a friend of his, who had never *left* [*divided himself from*] his side, interrogated him if before dying he had anything to communicate to his son: "If he *becomes*[13] a worthy man," answered Phocion, "tell him that I command him to forget the injustice of the Athenians:" such were his last accents.

[1] si debba. [2] illibata. [3] schiude. [4] cupo bisbiglio. [5] leggiero. [6] si vorrebbero avvolti. [7] comitiva. [8] vi fu chi giunse perfino. [9] si ristrinse. [10] turpi. [11] nappo. [12] cicuta. [13] sarà.

[2], [10] Used only in a *moral* sense. What Eng. word does turpe suggest? [4] Cupo = hollow; hence *dark, deep,* in colour; *dull, muttering,* in sound; *taciturn, reserved,* in character. [11] A term confined to the noble style.

99. ONE INSENSIBLE TO PAIN [THE INSENSIBLE] THROUGH
VIRTUE.

The philosopher Epictetus was slave *to [of]* a brutal
man by name Epaphroditus. The latter *struck*[1] vio-
lently *one of his legs;* and the good man, having-turned to him placidly the *eye* [brow], "Mind," he said,
"not to break it." That *inhuman man*[2], in place of
desisting, redoubled the blow, and it was such that he
broke it. Epictetus, without giving a sign either of
anger or of pain, added: "*I told you, you know*[3], that
you would have broken it."

[1]percosse. [2]disumano. [3]vel dissi già.

[3]Of course già is here an expletive.

---

100 THE PORTABLE INSCRIPTION.

It is known[1] that the great artists neglect not to
insert their own name in their works. All the *revenge*[2]
which Crates *of [from]* Thebes took *for [of]* an unjust
blow received from Nicodromus, through which his
forehead had remained *bruised*[3], was to fasten under
the *bruise*[4] a *ticket*[5] with this inscription: *Nicodromus fecit*[6].

[1]è noto. [2]vendetta. [3]illividita. [4]lividura. [5]cartellina. [6]fece.

[3], [4]From livido.

PROPER NAMES.

[Such names as are not included in this list are the same in Italian as in English.]

Achilles . . .	Achille
Actium . . .	Azio
Ælius	Elio
Æschines . . .	Eschine
Africanus . . .	Africano
Agamemnon .	Agamennone
Alexander . .	Alessandro
Algerine . . .	Algerino
Algiers . . .	Algeri
Alphonso . . .	Alfonso
Antioch . . .	Antiochia
Antipater . .	Antipatro
Antoninus . .	Antonino
Ardisheer Babe-	Ardochir Bade-
gan	gen
Arragon . . .	Aragona
Arsaces . . .	Arsace
Athenais . . .	Atenaide
Athenian . . .	Ateniese
Athens . . .	Atene
Augustus . . .	Augusto
Aurelius . . .	Aurelio
Austrian . . .	Austriaco
Avignon . . .	Avignone
Bastille . . .	Bastiglia
Berlin	Berlino
Bertrand . . .	Bertrando
Cœdicius . . .	Cecidio
Cæsar	Cesare
Caligula . . .	Caligola

Capitol . . .	Campidoglio
Carthaginian .	Cartaginese
Caspian . . .	Caspio
Cassander . .	Cassandro
Catherine . .	Caterina
Chang-hi . . .	Cang-hi
Charles . . .	Carlo
Chæronea . .	Cheronea
Chinese . . .	Cinese, Chinese
Christian . . .	Cristiano
Claudius . . .	Claudio
Commodus . .	Comodo
Constance . .	Costanza
Constantinople .	Costantinopoli
Crates	Crate
Crinitus . . .	Crinito
Ctesiphon . .	Ctesifone
Danube . . .	Danubio
Demaratus . .	Demarato
Demosthenes .	Demostene
East Indies . .	Indie orientali
Edward . . .	Eduardo
Egypt	Egitto
Elizabeth . . .	Elisabetta
England . . .	Inghilterra
English . . .	Inglese
Englishman . .	Inglese
Enguerrand . .	Enguerrando
Epaphroditus .	Epafrodito
Epictetus . . .	Epitteto
Ernest . . .	Ernesto

Eubulus	. . .	Eobolo	Leipsic . . .	Lipsia
Europe	. . .	Europa	Lille	Lilla
European	. .	Europeo	London . . .	Londra
Eustace	. . .	Eustachio	Lorraine . . .	Lorena
			Louis	Luigi
Flavius	. . .	Flavio	Lucius . . .	Lucio
Florence	. . .	Firenze	Luxembourg .	Lussemburgo
Florentine	. .	Fiorentino		
France	. . .	Francia	Macedonian . .	Macedone
Francis	. . .	Francesco	Mecænas . . .	Mecenate
Frank	. . .	Franco	Marcus . . .	Marco
Frederick	. . .	Federico	Margaret . . .	Margherita
French	. . .	Francese	Marseilles . .	Marsiglia
Frenchwoman	.	Francese	Martinique . .	Martinica
			Metellus . . .	Metello
Galienus	. . .	Galieno	Metius	Mezio
Gascon	. . .	Guascone	Milan	Milano
Gentile	. . .	Gentile	Montmorency ·	Montmorenci
George	. . .	Giorgio	Moorish . . .	Moro
German	. . .	Tedesco	Moscow . . .	Mosca
Germany	. . .	Germania	Moses	Mosè, Moisè
Goth	. . . .	Goto	Mussulman . .	Musulmano
Grecinus	. . .	Grecino		
Greece	. . .	Grecia	Naples	Napoli
Greek	. . . .	Greco	Narbonne . .	Narbona
Gustavus	. . .	Gustavo	Neapolitan . .	Napoletano
			Nicodromus . .	Nicodromo
Henry	. . . .	Enrico		
Heraclitus	. .	Eraclito	Octavius . . .	Ottavio
Holland	. . .	Olanda	Oliver	Oliviero
Hungary	. . .	Ungheria	Ottoman . . .	Ottomano
Indies	. . . .	Indie	Palatine . . .	Palatino
Invalides	. . ·	Invalidi	Papinianus . .	Papiniano
Italy	. . . .	Italia	Paris	Parigi
			Parthian . . .	Parto
James	. . . .	Giacomo	Pertinax . . .	Pertinace
Jew	. . . .	Ebreo, Giudeo	Peter	Pietro
John	. . . .	Giovanni	Petersburg . .	Pietroburgo
Joseph	. . .	Giuseppe	Philip	Filippo
Julius	. . . .	Giulio	Philipsburg . .	Filisburgo
			Phocion . . .	Focione
Kaffir	. . . .	Cafro	Piedmontese .	Piemontese
			Pius	Pio
Lanuvium	. .	Lanuvio	Poland . . .	Polonia
Latin	. . . .	Latino	Pomposianus .	Pomposiano
Leæna	. . .	Leonessa	Pont Royal · .	Ponte reale
			Portugal . . .	Portogallo

Portuguese	. . Portoghese		Swedish	. . . Svezzese
Probus	. . . Probo		Syria	. . . . Siria
Provence	. . . Provenza			
Prussian	. . . Prussiano		Tacitus	. . . Tacito
Publius	. . . Publio		Tartar	. . . . Tartaro
Punic	. . . . Punico		Teutonic	. . . Teutonico
			Thebes	. . . Tebe
Quaker	. . . Quacchero		Theodosius	. . Teodosio
Quintilian	. . Quintiliano		Theresa	. . . Teresa
			Thersites	. . Tersite
Rhodes	. . . Rodi		Titus	. . . . Tito
Rodomont	. . Rodomonte		Trajan	. . . . Traiano
Roman	. . . Romano		Turenne	. . . Turrena
Rome	. . . . Roma		Turin	. . . . Torino
			Turk	. . . . Turco
Saladin	. . . Saladino		Tuscany	. . . Toscana
Sassanid	. . . Sassanide			
Saxony	. . . Sassonia		Ulpius	. . . Ulpio
Scipio	. . . . Scipione			
Scotch	. . . Scozzese		Valentinian	. . Valentiniano
Seine	. . . . Senna		Venice	. . . Venezia
Seville	. . . Siviglia		Verus	. . . . Vero
Silvanus	. . . Silvano		Vespasian	. . Vespasiano
Socrates	. . . Socrate			
Spaniard	. . . Spagnuolo		Wales	. . . . Galles
Spanish	. . . Spagnuolo		Weser	. . . . Veser
Spartan	. . . Spartano		William	. . . Guglielmo
Strasburg	. . Strasburgo			
Sweden	. . . Svezia		Xenocrates	. . Senocrate

INDEX TO THE NOTES.

The figures refer to the pages.

I. Italian Words.

II. English, French and German Words.

(The French words are in italics, the German in the proper character.)

INDEX TO RULES.

Those who use this book are requested first to make
the following corrections:

PAGE.	LINE.			
59	2	*for*	Èrisanato	*read* È risanato.
72	last but one of text	„	*officer was the*	„ officer was the.
89	note 34	„	first	„ fist.
102	8	„	surpose	„ purpose.
110	3	„	else than	„ *else than.*
—	note 3 *before*		mi	*insert* nè.
123	7 of text	*for*	might point out	*read might point out*[2].
128	10			*erase* he.
130	14 fr. bottom	„	managed	*read managed.*
147	3	„	*caused*	„ caused.
151	16 fr. bottom	„	M. M.	„ MM
152	2	„	to	„ of.
—	11 fr. bottom	„	her	„ *her.*
153	2 fr. bottom	„	note of hand	„ *note of hand.*
158	5	„	*adness*	„ sadness.
159	2	„	an account of	„ *on account of.*
172	11 fr. bottom	*after*	Arrived	*insert* that he was.

Düben, printed by W . Steinmüller.

For EU product safety concerns, contact us at Calle de José Abascal, 56–1°,
28003 Madrid, Spain or eugpsr@cambridge.org.

www.ingramcontent.com/pod-product-compliance
Ingram Content Group UK Ltd.
Pitfield, Milton Keynes, MK11 3LW, UK
UKHW012346130625
459647UK00009B/573